A Guitar Maker's Manual

Jim Williams

First Printing April 1986
Second Printing August 1987
Third Printing July 1990

ISBN 978-0-9589075-0-7

Published by,

GUITARCRAFT

10 Albury St.,
Dudley.
N.S.W.   2290
Australia.

Exclusively distributed throughout the World by

Hal Leonard Publishing Corporation
7777 West Bluemound Road P.O. Box 13819 Milwaukee, WI 53213

Preface.

When the idea of writing a book on guitar making was presented to me several years ago, I had many reasons for being reluctant to undertake such a project. One of the main reasons was the number of books on the subject already available, especially considering the limited readership. What finally prompted me to go ahead was the fact that I felt something was lacking in the approach taken by many writers on the subject. Writing technical books is not to be taken lightly and I was greatly inspired by Roger Siminoff's *Constructing a Bluegrass Mandolin* and John Muir's *How to Keep Your Volkswagen Alive* because they adopt a step by step approach that is both practical and easy to follow. This is what I have endeavoured to do.

This is not a "Build a Guitar One Rainy Weekend" book, but a method of constructing an acoustic steel string or nylon string guitar that should result in an instrument which is appealing in both sound and appearance. One of the main ingredients required is patience, another is perserverance. The time it takes to construct the special jigs described will be more than rewarded as these help you maintain control over the process and produce a consistent result. Avoid the temptation to rush ahead, read each chapter carefully before commencing work on that section; also, develop the self discipline to repeat any part of the process you're not satisfied with as you're going to have live with these faults for a long time. Having said that I should also warn against having too great an expection, skills are developed over time so don't be too critical of your first effort.

The method I have laid out is adapted from that which I have used to guide many students through their first guitar. It is the product of what I was taught, coupled with my years of experience in guitar construction and repair plus the input of my fellow luthiers whose knowledge has been shared unselfishly on many occasions.

I trust that you will derive as much satisfaction from guitar making as I do.

Acknowledgements.

This book would never have happened without the following people;

Richard and Mary Williams, my parents, who always supported and encouraged my interest in the guitar.

Ray Johnson, my first guitar teacher, whose enthusiasm for the instrument proved infectious.

Toni Jones, who encouraged and supported my desire to become a guitar maker.

Robin Moyes, a good friend as well as being the first guitar maker I ever met and a constant source of inspiration.

George Morris, who taught me guitar making and instilled an enthusiasm that has endured.

Charles Fox, who organised the course in guitar making that changed my life.

Mike Davidson and Richard Widows, who believed in me at the beginning.

My fellow luthiers, Gerard Gilet, Teen Goh, Dan Kellaway, Graham McDonald, Peter Richardson and Greg Smallman, all of whom have contributed in some way to my methods of work and some of whom browbeat me into writing this book.

Friends, aquaintances and ex-students who assisted in many subtle ways.

A special thank you to Robin Moyes for his assistance with the chapter on finishing, Graham McDonald for modelling for the photographs, and Tony Nicholls for his advice and assistance in the production of the book.

Thank you all!

Contents

Full size template diagrams are contained in an envelope inside the back cover.

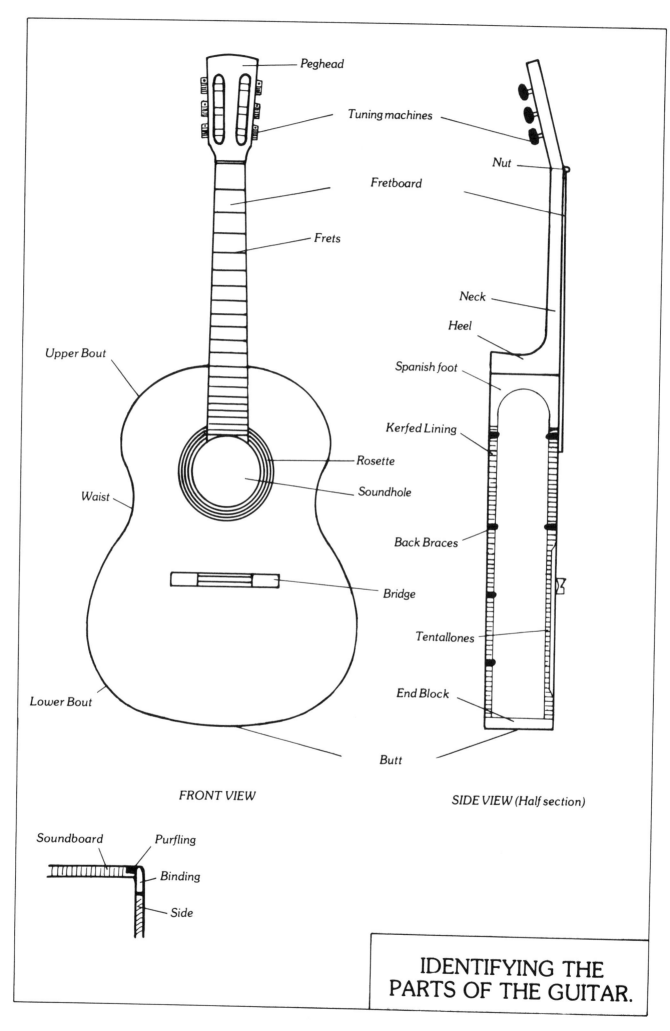

Peghead

Tuning machines

Nut

Fretboard

Frets

Neck

Heel

Upper Bout

Spanish foot

Kerfed Lining

Waist

Rosette

Soundhole

Back Braces

Bridge

Tentallones

Lower Bout

End Block

Butt

FRONT VIEW

SIDE VIEW (Half section)

Soundboard   Purfling

Binding

Side

IDENTIFYING THE
PARTS OF THE GUITAR.

i

Glossary of Terms.

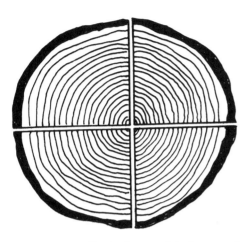

The log is sawn into four quarters

Planks are sawn from each face alternately.

QUARTER SAWN

Diagram # 2

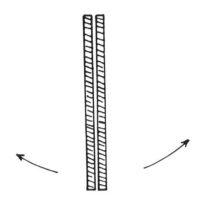

Opens like a book

The grain of the two boards is matched

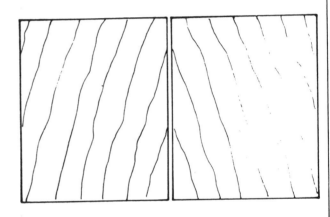

BOOKMATCHED

Diagram # 1

Neck Relief: Is the slight curve along the neck, the purpose of which is to facillitate free vibration of the string. It is measured by placing a 12" (300mm) rule between the 1st and 12th frets and checking the clearance at the 5th fret. This is done with the strings at full tension.

Compensation: As a string is fretted, it is stretched and raised slightly in pitch. In order to compensate for this the bridge saddle is moved further toward the butt. This increases the effective string length and lowers the pitch slightly. The amount of compensation required varies with the guage and tension of the string. Nylon strings are of much lower tension and are generally not compensated.

Bookmatched: Refers to two pieces of timber which have been adjacent to each other in a board and are then opened out for use. (See diagram # 1).

Quartersawn: This is the practice of sawing a log into quarters and then resawing boards from each of the sawn faces. This yeilds wood in which the grain is close to vertical. (See diagram # 2). Quartersawn timber is less susceptible to warping or cupping as it dries.

Action: Is the distance between the top of the fret and the bottom of the string and is usually measured at the 12th fret.

Suppliers:

There are many reputable suppliers of guitar maker's materials in Europe and North America, though precious few in Australia. The following list includes one from each area all of whom provide a local and international mail order service. I have dealt with each of these suppliers and can recommend them in terms of service and range of materials available. The ommission of a supplier in no way represents a value judgement.

U.S.A.

Luthiers Mercantile,
P.O. Box 774,
Healdsburg,
California   95448,
U.S.A.
Phone (707) 433 1823.

Wood, tools, hardware, finishing materials, books, glue etc.
They have a wonderful catologue; send US$3.00 plus postage.

Australia.

Guitar Woods,
34a Beatrice St.
Balgowlah,
N.S.W.   2093,
Australia.
Phone for appointment (02) 94 3638.

Wood, glue, purfling and binding etc.
They also provide a resawing, thickness sanding and fret slotting service.

Great Britain.

David Dyke Luthier's Supplies,
The Hall,
Horebeech Lane,
Heathfield,
East Sussex,
U.K.   TN 21 OHR.

Wood, purflings and bindings, glue, hardware etc.
Write for price list.

Sources:

If you wish to learn more about guitar making the following sources are worthwhile checking.

If you wish to pursue musical instrument making in any form I heartily recommend that you join the Guild of American Luthiers, an organisation with many functions, the most important being an information network. Invaluable!

Guild of American Luthiers,
8222 South Park Ave.
Tacoma,
Washington   98408,
U.S.A.

Australian Association of Musical Instrument Makers,
35 Day Rd.,
Cheltenham,
N.S.W.   2119

Frets Magazine,
Subscription Dept.,
P.O. Box 2120
Cupertino,
California.   95014,
U.S.A.

Tools, Timbers and Materials

Tools.

While machine tools are not an absolute necessity they can be very useful in terms of achieving a consistent result, as well as saving time. I prefer to work with a minimum of machine tools because I enjoy the feel of working wood with hand tools. However, there are a number of machine tools that would be hard to live without.

A small bandsaw 12" or 14" (300 or 350mm).
A drill press (sometimes called a bench drill).
A 1 horsepower router.
A small electric hand drill.
A Dremel moto-tool.

Obviously, no-one is going to rush out and buy a band saw and a drill press to build their first guitar. However, access to such things can be gained by enrolling in a part-time woodworking class. These classes are conducted in most major cities and large country centres, usually in conjunction with the local high school. Teachers of these classes are generally quite interested in unusual projects and very helpful.

The following is a list of basic hand tools that I work with;

Combination fine india/coarse sharpening stone.

A piece of leather for stropping.
Block plane.
No. 4 smoothing plane.
Flat spokeshave.
Cabinetmakers chisels 3/16 " (5mm), ½" (12.5mm) and 1" (25mm).
Bent chisel ¾" (19mm).
X-acto or similar hobby knife.
1mm cabinet scraper.
Four 6" (150mm) sash cramps.
Four 4" (100mm) cam clamps.
Six 6" (150mm) cam clamps.
Six various size small G cramps.
Fine tooth hobby hacksaw.
Dovetail saw to cut a 0.025" (0.6mm) kerf.
Tenon saw.
Coping saw.
12" (300mm) flat smooth file.
6" (150mm) three cornered file.

Carpenters pincers.
Combination pliers.
Standard size fret file.
Nut files (needle files can be substituted).
Small tapered reamer.
12" (300mm) steel rule.
6" (150mm) steel engineers rule.
0 — 0.125" (0 — 6.35mm) dial gauge.
Carpenters hammer.
Hard rubber painter's sanding block.
File card (wire brush for cleaning files).
Honing guide.
Honing oil or nearsfoot oil.
Plumbers gas torch (for bending the sides).
Circle cutter.
Vise. (I have a preference for using a brand called Versa-Vise which is made in the U.S.A. A swivelling engineers vise fitted with deep wooden jaws will suffice).

Most of the above items are available at a tool specialist or a good hardware store. Special tools such as fret files, nut files, and cam clamps will have to be purchased from a luthier's supply outlet. (See List of Suppliers).

Tool Maintenance;

The bottom line of good craftsmanship is sharp tools. It is almost impossible to produce neat, accurate work with a dull chisel, plane or knife. Sharpen tools frequently, the few minutes it takes will save hours of frustration.
Planes and chisels have a grinding angle of 25° and a honing angle of 30°. Most new tools are supplied ground but not honed.
The honing angle is obtained by setting up the blade in the appropriate section of the honing guide, applying a few drops of honing oil on the fine india stone, and moving the blade along its surface in a few firm forward strokes (see photo # 1). A burr will form on the edge (see diagram # 2) and this should be removed on the leather strop. A sharp chisel or plane blade should shave hair from your arm with ease (without shaving cream).

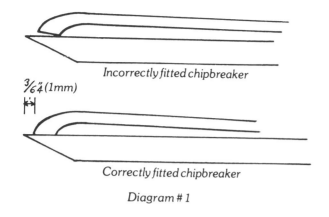

Incorrectly fitted chipbreaker

$\frac{3}{64}$ (1mm)

Correctly fitted chipbreaker

Diagram # 1

Photo #1

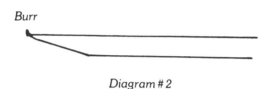

Burr

Diagram # 2

Setting Up a Smoothing Plane;

The sole of the plane is unlikely to be level,when purchased new. To true the sole,first dismantle the plane by removing the blade,frog and chipbreaker. The sole should then be rubbed over fine emery cloth glued to a sheet of flat glass until all uneveness dissappears.

Check that the chipbreaker fits correctly,if not file until its front edge contacts the blade (see diagram # 1). The chipbreaker should be tightened so that it rests about $\frac{3}{64}$ (1.2mm) back from the edge of the blade.

Additional Items;

GLUE: I prefer to use aliphatic resin glue for all glueing on the guitar. There are a number of brands available but I use Franklins Titebond (made in the U.S.A.) almost exclusively. The acid test for a guitar making glue is the glueing of the bridge so don't use cheap PVA's which have poor creep strength.

RUBBER CEMENT; For glueing sandpaper to the sanding blocks.

POSTERBOARD; For cutting out templates,protectors etc.

(Rubber cement and posterboard are available from art supply shops).

SANDPAPER; 1.) Aluminium oxide fre-cut or no-fil; 5 sheets each of 60,120,180 and 320 grit.
　　　　　　 2.) Wet or dry; 1 sheet of 400 and 5 sheets each of 800 1200 grit.

DOWEL STICKS; Twelve 40" (about 1metre) lengths of $\frac{5}{16}$ (8mm) dowel.
　　　　　　 A 80" (about 2metres) length of 1½" (38mm) dowel. (For dowel clamps).

DOWEL CLAMPS; An 80" (about 2metres) length of 1½" (38mm) dowel.
　　　　　　 A 40" (about 1metre) length of ¼" threaded rod.
　　　　　　 Eighteen ¼" wing nuts.
　　　　　　 Eighteen ¼" washers.

THREADED ROD SETS; 40" (about 1metre) of ⅜" threaded rod.
　　　　　　 Eight ⅜" wing nuts.
　　　　　　 Eight ⅜" hexagon nuts.
　　　　　　 Sixteen ⅜" washers.

PLYWOOD; One sheet 4' X 2' X ¾" (1200 X 600 X 19) hardwood ply (don't use cheap ply or particle board as this is for the workboard).
　　　　　　 One sheet 6' X 3' X ½" (1800 X 900 X 12.5mm) for jigs.

COPPER PIPE; 3" (75mm) diameter,10" (250mm) long with end cap and bracket.(For side bending).

STAINLESS STEEL; Two sheets of 24 guage 6" X 32" (150 X 820mm).

Six lengths of hardwood 24" X 2" X 1" (600 X 50 X 25mm), plus three wedges 24" X 1" (600 X 25mm), 3" (75mm) at one end tapering to zero at the other. (For the soundboard, and back, jointing jig).

Timbers

The Soundboard:

The choice of timber for the soundboard is quite obviously critical as this determines, to a large extent, the tone colour of the instrument.

For a classic guitar it is preferable to use western red cedar or European spruce. Western red cedar has become increasingly popular though it is slightly more difficult to work due to its softer nature. I recommend western red cedar for a first instrument.

For a steel string guitar, sitka spruce is the most commonly used. However, I have used both western red cedar and European spruce with considerable success. I again recommend western red cedar for a first instrument.

Back and Sides:

For a classic guitar the traditional choice is either East Indian or Brazilian rosewood. A number of makers use flamed or curly maple with great success. I recommend East Indian rosewood for a first instrument.

For a steel string guitar the traditional timbers are Honduras mahogany, curly maple and either East Indian or Brazilian rosewood. I have seen many other timbers used with excellent results, including koa, North American black walnut, padauk and New Guinea rosewood (the last two are related species). Australian natives such as Tasmanian blackwood (an acacia, related to koa) and tulip satinwood are most suitable. I recommend mahogany for a first instrument.

The Neck:

For a classic guitar the traditional choice is Spanish cedar. However, Honduras mahogany, sapele and Queensland maple work very well. I recommend Spanish cedar for a first instrument

as it is easier to work and gives off a wonderful aroma when sanded or planed.

For a steel string guitar Honduras mahogany is the most popular choice and with good reason. It is relatively light and very stable. Queensland maple is excellent for the same reasons. Sapele, curly maple and rock maple are suitable but more difficult to work. I recommend Honduras mahogany for a first instrument.

The Fretboard:

Gaboon ebony is the favoured timber due to its hardness and solid black colour. Macassar ebony is less favoured due, in the main, to its lighter colour which is often streaked with brown or grey. Brazilian and East Indian rosewoods make excellent fretboards but do not wear as well. I recommend rosewood for a first guitar.

The Bridge:

A lot of makers use ebony and feel that the bridge and fretboard should be of matching timbers. I don't subscribe to this line of thought preferring to use Brazilian rosewood. East Indian rosewood works well and this is my recommendation for a first instrument.

Binding:

This is where we enter the rather nebulous area of aesthetics. My rule of thumb is to use maple binding on dark coloured back and sides (e.g. rosewood) and rosewood binding on light coloured wood (e.g. Mahogany).

Purfling:

To add definition to the shape of the guitar it is preferable to use purfling of some description around the soundboard, especially when using light coloured binding. This can take the form of simple black/white strips, which are suitable for both classic and steel string guitars, or herringbone, half herringbone etc. for a steel string guitar. I recommend a simple black/white/black strip for a classic guitar and either herringbone or black/white/black for a steel string guitar.

Humidity.

One of the problems facing all woodworkers is humidity. Wood is a hygroscopic material, which means it takes on or sheds moisture according to its environment; this in turn causes the wood to expand or contract. These changes usually effect conifers (softwoods) more rapidly than hardwoods.

What this means to the guitar maker is that all glueing of parts, in particular the soundboard bracing, should be carried out in an environment of less than 60% humidity. This should be monitored several times a day using a wet and dry bulb thermometer or a hygroscope. If you don't wish to go to the expense of buying one of these instruments, most radio stations give humidity readings with their weather reports. If you live in a big city, phone the weather bureau.

If the soundboard (and in extreme cases, the back and sides) is glued in a high humidity environment there is a real danger that cracks will develop along the grain when the guitar is left for a few hours in a low humidity environment. This problem is most extreme in houses with central heating, where the humidity falls below 10%.

Materials

For a Steel String Guitar:

SOUNDBOARD: Two bookmatched pieces of western red cedar 22″ X 8″ (550 X 200mm).

BACK: Two bookmatched pieces of Honduras mahogany 22″ X 8″ (550 X 200mm).

SIDES: Two bookmatched pieces of Honduras mahogany 32″ X 5″ (820 X 125mm).

NECK: One piece of Honduras mahogany 24″ X 3″ X ¾″ (600 X 75 X 19mm).

HEEL BLOCK: One piece of Honduras mahogany 6″ X 3″ X 4″ (150 X 75 X 100mm).

FRETBOARD: One piece of East Indian rosewood 18″ X 2½″ X 5/16″ (450 X 63 X 8mm).

BRACE STOCK:Two blocks of sitka spruce approximately 24″ X 2″ X 2″ (600 X 50 X 50mm).

BRIDGE: One piece of East Indian or Brazilian rosewood 7″ X 1½″ X ⅜″ (175 X 38 X 10mm)

END BLOCK: One piece of ½″ (12.5mm) good quality plywood, 5″ X 2″ (125 X 50mm).

HEADSTOCK VENEERS: All pieces at least 8″ X 3″ (200 X 75mm).
One piece of ebony veneer 0.03″ (0.7mm) thick,
One piece of holly or maple veneer 0.03″ (0.7mm) thick,
One piece of rosewood 5/64″ (2.0mm) thick.

BINDINGS: Five pieces of East Indian rosewood 32″ X 3/32″ X ¼″ (820 X 2.4 X 6mm).

PURFLINGS: Three pieces of herringbone or six pieces of black/white 32″ (820mm) long.

ADDITIONAL ITEMS:
A piece of holly or maple veneer (for the upper bout inside) 0.03″ thick and 3″ X 13″ (0.7 X 75 X 425mm).
A piece of rosewood for the heel cap 1½″ X ½″ X ¼″ (38 X 12.5 X 6.35mm).
A length of 3/16″ mild steel rod 32″ (820mm) long.
A 3/16″ 32 t.p.i. allen nut (for the truss rod).
4 Feet (1.2metres) of standard fretwire.
A bone nut blank.
A bone compensated saddle blank.
Six bridge pins.
A set of tuning machines.

For a Classic Guitar:

SOUNDBOARD: Two bookmatched pieces of western red cedar 22″ X 7½″ (550 X 190mm).

BACK: Two bookmatched pieces of East Indian rosewood 22″ X 7½″ (550 X 190mm).

SIDES: Two bookmatched pieces of East Indian rosewood 32″ X 4″ (820 X 100mm).

NECK: One piece of Spanish cedar 24″ X 3″ X ¾″ (600 X 75 X 19mm).

HEEL BLOCK: One piece of Spanish cedar 6″ X 3″ X 4″ (150 X 75 X 100mm).

BRACE STOCK: Two blocks of European spruce 24″ X 2″ X 2″ (600 X 50 X 50mm).

ADDITIONAL ITEMS:
Classic guitar rosette. Bone nut blank. Bone saddle blank.

The remaining materials are the same as for a steel string guitar, ommitting the truss rod, bridge pins and herringbone purfling. Maple binding are substituted for rosewood.

The
Soundboard

The Soundboard:

The soundboard is also referred to as the top, the face, the front etc. However, I prefer the term soundboard as this is where the essential sound character of the instrument is developed. Antonio Juan de Torres, the famous Spanish luthier, was so emphatic on this point that he constructed a guitar with papier mache back and sides to illustrate it.

The criteria are essentially the same whether you are making a steel string or nylon string guitar. When selecting suitable timber the following qualities are preferable.

A. The two pieces should be bookmatched.

B. The timber should be quarter sawn.

C. There should be a high number of annular rings per inch (per 25mm). More than 15 in the case of western red cedar, and more than 10 in the case of spruce.

D. Medullary rays (also referred to as silking) should be apparent, although this is usually only visible on planed surfaces.

E. Stiffness is a quality allied to **B** and **C** and can be tested by flexing the timber across the grain. Keep in mind that the stiffness will vary according to the thickness of the timber and don't flex too vigorously.

F. Tap tone is basically a combination of **B, C, D** and **E** and is tested by holding one piece of wood between thumb and forefinger about a quarter of the way down one edge and tapping near the centre with a knuckle of the other hand (see diagram # 1). Tapping the wood should produce a clear, resonant, almost bell-like tone. Recognising good tap tone is a comparative thing and will become more apparent with experience.

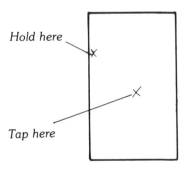

Diagram # 1

Hold here

Tap here

Joining the Soundboard.

NOTE: It is most important that this joint be well executed.

A. Select the edges of the soundboard halves with the closest grain and make these the edges to be joined. When making this selection take into account flaws in the timber.

B. With the two pieces taped together, roughly true the glueing edge with a plane on the shooting board (see photo # 1). A No. 4 smoothing is satisfactory for this task although a jointing plane is more efficient.

Photo # 1

C. Using a spirit level with 80 grit sandpaper glued to one edge, completely true the edges (see photo # 2).

Photo # 2

D. Test the quality of the join by holding the two pieces of timber edge to edge in front of a strong light source (see photo # 3). No light should be visible when the join is ready to glue.

Photo # 3

E. Set up dry in the jointing jig to ensure a good fit. The twine should be wound in figure of 8 patterns, lightly secured and the wedges fitted (see photo # 4).

Photo # 4

NOTE: Setting up joints dry, before glueing, is a good habit to develop.

IMPORTANT: Before applying glue, be sure to wax the jig where it is likely to contact the glued surfaces. Failure to do so can have embarrassing and annoying consequences.

F. Run a glue line along one true edge and set up in the jig as in step **E.**

At this point it is advisable to leave the soundboard at least two days to allow the moisture to completely dry from the glue join. In the meantime you can proceed with the neck.

Thicknessing the Soundboard;

A. Remove the soundboard from the jig.
B. Using a cabinet scraper, scrape away the excess glue from the centre join.
C. Clamp the soundboard to the bench with a clamp at each end of one edge. Lightly test plane one side to determine grain direction.

NOTE: The bench top must be flat.

D. By planing with the grain, roughly level each side of the soundboard (see photo # 5).

Photo # 5

E. Select the side with the least flaws and sand flat using the large sanding block with 120 grit sandpaper. This will be the outside of the soundboard. (See photo # 6).

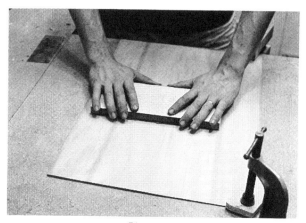

Photo # 6

NOTE: don't use sandpaper more coarse than 120 grit on the surface of the soundboard.

F. Measure the thickness of the soundboard at various points using the thickness guage, and mark the readings lightly with a pencil, as you make them, on the unsanded surface of the soundboard (see photo # 7).

Photo # 7

G. Plane the inside of the soundboard in stages, checking and marking the thickness frequently. Continue planing until the soundboard is around 0.125" (3.2mm) for a steel string guitar and 0.100" (2.5mm) for a nylon string guitar.
H. Sand the inside flat using the large sanding block and 120 grit sandpaper.

NOTE: Make sure the bench is clean from here on to prevent damage to the soundboard.

Making the Rosette;

Rosettes for classic guitars are complex and time consuming to make so I suggest purchasing these, at least until your guitar making skills are developed. Steel string guitar rosettes can be purchased but they are relatively simple to make. It is usual with steel string guitars to have the rosette match the soundboard purfling be it herringbone, half-herringbone, black/white/black or whatever.

A. Make a circle from ⅛" (3mm) acrylic sheet. The diameter of the circle should be ¼" larger than the diameter of the soundhole.

B. If using herringbone, or other complex patterns, soak a 16" (400mm) length of the purfling in very hot (not boiling) water in a soaking tray or tub for ten to fifteen minutes.

C. Split the purfling near its centre using a dull knife. Make sure that the knife follows the same line right through otherwise the rosette will be uneven and lumpy. (See photo #

D. Smear glue on each adjoining piece of the rosette and bend around the plastic circle using masking tape to hold it in position. It isn't necessary that the circle be complete as the resulting gap should be covered by the fretboard. The rosette should be left to dry overnight.

Photo # 8

Fitting the Rosette;

A. Lightly mark the centre join on the outside of the soundboard using a soft sharp pencil. Then, using the full body template, mark the outline of the guitar body on both sides of the soundboard and mark the position of the soundhole.

B. Drill a ¼" (6.35mm) hole in the centre of the soundhole position. Use a piece of scrap wood as backing to prevent grain tearout and holes in the bench. A dowelling, or spur, bit is best for this as it is easier to centre and gives a cleaner cut.

C. Using the square workboard held in a vise, line up the hole in the soundboard with the hole in the workboard and clamp in position. (Use cam clamps if available).

D. Using either a circle cutter or the router with adjustable trammel, cut the trench for the rosette about ⅛" (3mm) outside the soundhole line and about half the thickness of the soundboard. On classic guitars be careful not to exceed the thickness of the rosette (see photos 9a & 9b).

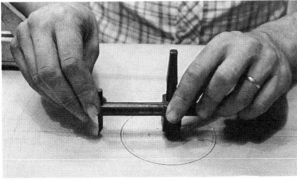
Photo # 9A

Photo # 9B

E. If using the router, simply keep adjusting the trammel and routing until the width of the slot is such that the rosette fits neatly, but not tightly. If using the circle cutter, make a second cut such that the two cuts are separated by the width of the rosette. Chisel out the slot to the required depth (see photo # 10).

NOTE: It is important that the rosette should not fit too tightly as the glue will cause the spruce, or cedar to swell and make fitting difficult, possibly damaging the soundboard.

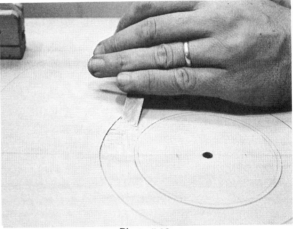
Photo # 10

F. Apply a liberal amount of glue to the rosette channel, fit the rosette and, using a piece of ⅛" (3mm) acrylic to spread the clamping pressure, clamp in position (see photo # 11).

Leave for a couple of days to dry completely.

Photo # 11

Levelling the Rosette and Cutting the Soundboard to Shape;

A. Trim the excess from the rosette using a chisel to roughly trim and then a cabinet scraper to level (see photo # 12).

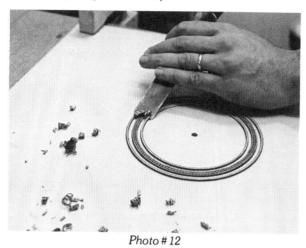

Photo # 12

B. Sand away all the excess glue and bring to final with 120 grit sandpaper on the large sanding block. It is important to use a large sanding block to avoid low spots around the rosette.

NOTE: Once the soundhole is cut it is unwise to attempt any further levelling in this area.

C. For steel string guitar only. Using either the circle cutter or the router cut out the soundhole with the soundboard mounted on the square workboard.

The classic guitar soundhole is cutout during the bracing of the soundboard.

D. Cut out the shape of the guitar on a bandsaw leaving about ⅛" (3mm) excess outside the line. If you don't have access to a bandsaw this can be done carefully with a coping saw using a scrap piece of thin plywood as support to prevent splitting along the grain.

E. Make a rough posterboard template the same size as the soundboard to use as a protector against damage to the outer surface.

Bracing the Soundboard;

The bracing requirements for steel string and nylon string guitars are radically different and I felt it easier to cover this in two separate sections.

Steel String Guitar;

The braces can be made from spruce or western red cedar and should be of quarter sawn timber ½" X ⅜" (12.5 X 9.5mm) with the grain perpendicular to the soundboard (see diagram # 2).

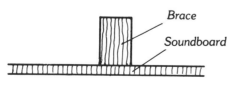

Brace

Soundboard

Diagram # 2

A. Mark the bracing pattern on the inside of the soundboard with a sharp, soft pencil.
B. Cut each brace to length.
C. Sand the glueing surface of each brace until flat. This is a little easier to accomplish if two are sanded together.
D. Make the joint on the main X braces (2A & 2B in diagram # 3). A snug fit here is important (see photo # 13).

Photo # 13

E. Drill a ¼" (6.35mm) hole in the centre of brace 1 (see diagram # 3).
F. Using GO sticks, set up the main X braces on the soundboard, dry. (See photo # 14).

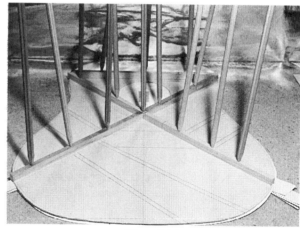

Photo # 14

NOTE: It is important to use the posterboard protector between the soundboard and GO stick board.

G. Disassemble and smear glue on the X brace joint and the glueing surface of the braces. Position correctly and clamp in place with GO sticks.

NOTE: The GO sticks shouldn't be closer than 3" (75mm) apart. In the interest of aesthetics, it is good practice to wipe away the excess glue with a scrap of posterboard.

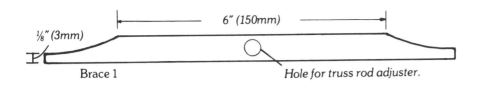

6" (150mm)

⅛" (3mm)

Brace 1

Hole for truss rod adjuster.

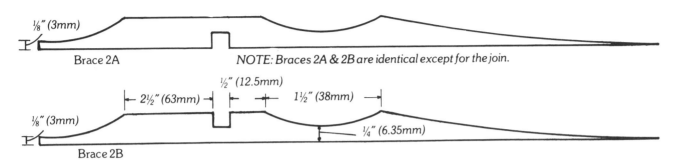

⅛" (3mm)

Brace 2A

NOTE: Braces 2A & 2B are identical except for the join.

½" (12.5mm)

2½" (63mm)

1½" (38mm)

⅛" (3mm)

¼" (6.35mm)

Brace 2B

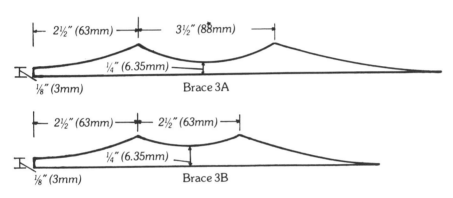

2½" (63mm)

3½" (88mm)

¼" (6.35mm)

⅛" (3mm)

Brace 3A

2½" (63mm)

2½" (63mm)

¼" (6.35mm)

⅛" (3mm)

Brace 3B

Peak at mid-point.

⅛" (3mm)

Braces 4A, B, C & D

Diagram # 3

H. The braces should be given at least an hour to dry (if using Titebond) then removed from the GO stick board, placed on the workboard and shaped. (See diagram # 3).

NOTE: When scalloping, cut a saw kerf in the centre of the scallop to the required depth and work from each end with a chisel. Tape a piece of posterboard each side of the brace to protect the soundboard when chiseling (see photo # 15). The braces can be sanded smooth with 120 grit sandpaper.

I. Glue brace 1 as above and, after drying, clamp to the soundboard and shape (see diagram # 3).
J. Repeat the process for braces 3A & 3B.
K. Repeat the process for braces 4A,B,C & D.
L. Glue a suitable piece of veneer on the upper section of the soundboard, adjoining brace 1 with its grain at 90° to the soundboard. Use a piece of ½" (12.5mm) particle board to distribute the GO stick pressure.
M. Make a bridge plate using a piece of rosewood or maple 0.100" (2.5mm) thick.
N. Glue the bridge plate in position using a piece of particle board to distribute the GO stick pressure.

Photo # 15

The soundboard is now complete.

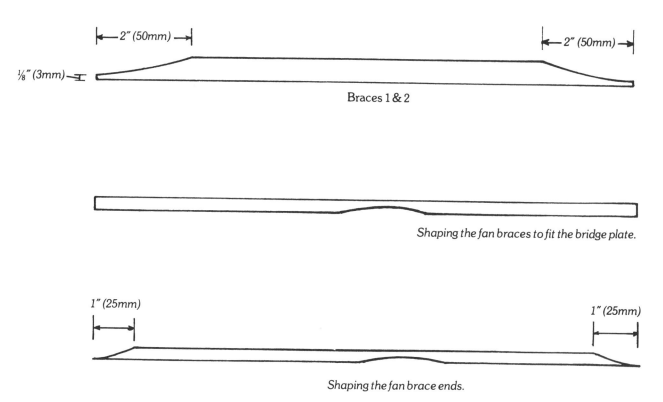

←2" (50mm)→   ←2" (50mm)→

⅛" (3mm)

Braces 1 & 2

Shaping the fan braces to fit the bridge plate.

1" (25mm)   1" (25mm)

Shaping the fan brace ends.

Diagram # 5

Nylon String Guitar: The braces are usually made from European spruce or western red cedar although sitka spruce is satisfactory. The timber should be quartersawn with the grain perpendicular to the soundboard.

NOTE: It is important to use the poster board protector from here on.

A. Mark the bracing pattern on the inside of the soundboard with an H.B. pencil.

B. Make braces 1 & 2 from ½" X ⅜" (12.5 X 9.5mm) vertical grain stock. Cut to length and sand the glueing surfaces flat.

C. Make fan braces 3 to 9 and braces 10 & 11 from ¼" X ⅜" vertical grain stock. Cut to length and ensure that the glueing surfaces are flat. Repeat for braces 12 & 13.

D. Make the bridge plate and soundhole reinforcement from soundboard offcuts. The grain of the bridge plate should run at 90° to the grain of the soundboard.

E. Glue the soundhole reinforcement in place using GO sticks and a piece of ½" (12.5mm) scrap to distribute the clamping pressure.

F. When dry, drill a ¼" (6.35mm) hole in the centre of the soundhole right through the reinforcing plate. Remount the soundboard on the square workboard, clamp firmly in position and, using a circle cutter or router, cut out the soundhole.

G. Shape the inside edge of the soundhole (see diagram # 4) using 120 grit sandpaper.

Diagram # 4

H. Clamp braces 1 & 2 dry with Go sticks and, when satisfied, glue in position. The GO sticks should be no closer than 3" (75mm) apart and any excess glue should be removed with a scrap of posterboard.

I. When dry shape the braces using a ½" (12.5mm) chisel (see diagram # 5).
Tape a piece of posterboard to each side of the brace for protection when chiseling.

J. Glue the bridge plate in position and leave at least an hour to dry.

K. Shape the bridge plate profile.

L. Fan braces 5,6 & 7 have to be shaped to fit neatly over the bridge plate before glueing (see diagram # 5 and photo # 16).

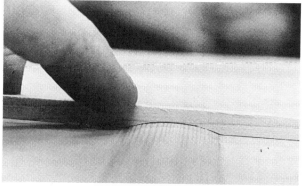

Photo # 16

M. Set up fan braces 5,6 &7 dry and clamp with GO sticks to ensure a snug fit. Remove,smear with glue and clamp in position.

N. Repeat this procedure for fan braces 3,4,8 & 9.

O. When all 7 fan braces are in position, shape (as per diagram # 5) using a ½" (12.5mm) chisel. Sand the edges smooth with 120 grit sandpaper. Tape a piece of posterboard ech side for protection.

P. Glue braces 10 & 11 in place and shape.

Q. Glue a piece of veneer to the soundboard above brace 1 with the grain at 90° to the grain of the soundboard. Use a piece of ½" particle board to distribute the GO stick pressure.

R. Trim the veneer to the shape of the soundboard when dry.

The soundboard is now complete (see photo # 17).

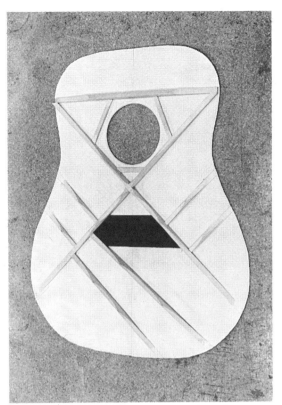

Completed steel string soundboard

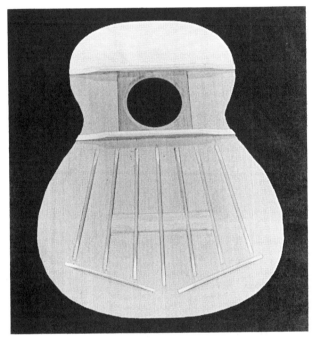

Photo # 17

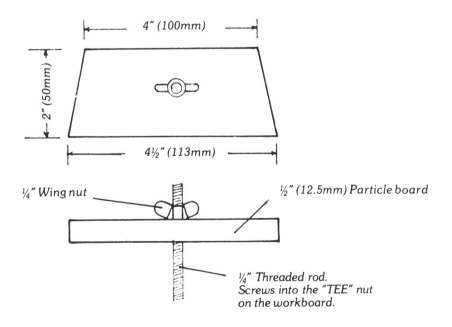

4" (100mm)

2" (50mm)

4½" (113mm)

¼" Wing nut

½" (12.5mm) Particle board

¼" Threaded rod. Screws into the "TEE" nut on the workboard.

SOUNDHOLE CLAMP

Notes:

The Neck

The Neck:

The methods I use for steel string and classic guitar necks are similar so I have noted the differences only where necessary.

A. True one flat surface of the neck blank using a smoothing plane or jointing plane and finally level with 80 grit sandpaper on the large sanding block. Check along its length with a straight edge (see photo # 1). This surface will be the back of the neck so it is important that it be true as all neck measurements are based on this.

Photo # 1

B. True one edge so that it is at 90° to the true surface and check along its length with a straight edge.
C. True the other edge so that the two are parallel and at 90° to the true surface.
D. Using a tri-square mark a line across the true surface 5" (125mm) from one end and mark an 18° angle on each edge of the neck blank. (See diagram # 1).

E. Mark a line on the rough side of the blank where the 18° lines meet its surface.
F. Using the lines as a guide, take a tenon saw and cut off the end of the neck blank. This off-cut will become the peghead (see photo # 2).

Photo # 2

G. True the rough surface of the peghead so that it is parallel to the original true surface.
H. True the angled surface of the peghead using a block plane then a small sanding block with 80 grit sandpaper. This surface will be glued to the back of the neck (see diagram # 1) and is called the peghead splice.
I. Set the peghead splice up dry, making sure to firmly clamp the end of each piece to prevent slipping when glue is applied. It is also a good idea to protect the surface of the wood with scrap timber. (See photo # 3).
J. Glue the peghead splice, allow at least an hour to dry, then remove from the clamps and mark out the neck taper and peghead thickness as in diagram # 1. Mark a centre line on the back of the neck and peghead.

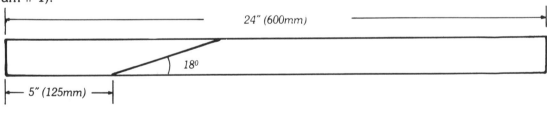

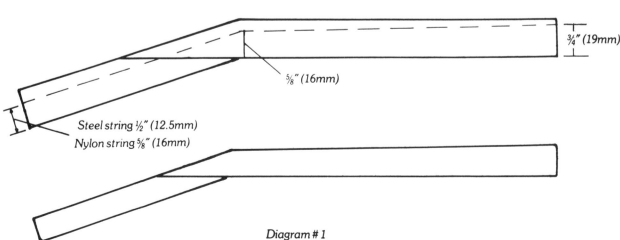

Diagram # 1

Photo # 3

K. Plane the neck taper down to its dimensions using a smoothing plane or a jointing plane. Sand to a true surface with 80 grit sandpaper on the large sanding block.

L. Repeat this process for the peghead.

NOTE: The next step applies to steel string guitar only.

M. For a steel string the truss rod slot should be cut down the centre of the upper surface of the neck. This slot should be 7/32" (5.5mm) wide by 13/32" (10mm) deep and stop approximately 1" (25mm) from the peghead.

Ma. Draw a centre line along the upper surface of the neck.

Mb. Set the router table up with a 3/16" (5mm) bit in the router and adjust the fence so that the slot will be cut along the centre of the neck. (See photo # 4). Mark the end of the slot on the back of the neck with a pencil, and mark the router fence where it aligns with the bit. Failure to do so means that you will have to resort to guesswork.

NOTE: 1. Wear a protective face shield or goggles when routing.

2. Don't attempt to route the slot to full depth in one as it may cause the bit to break.

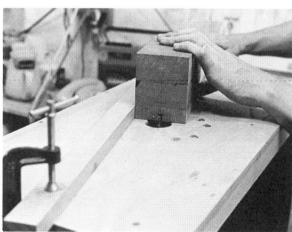

Photo # 4

Mc. When the slot is cut to full depth adjust the router fence to cut a slot wide enough to fit the truss rod plus the thickness of its tape wrapping 7/32" (5.5mm).

Md. To cut the slot by hand, first mark a line 7/64" (2.8mm) either side of the centre line of the neck.

Me. Clamp a straight edge so that it aligns with one of these lines. Using the straight edges as a guide make several deep cuts with a sharp knife along its length stopping 1" (25mm) from the peghead splice. Repeat this process for the other side of the slot. (See photo # 5).

Photo # 5

Mf. Remove the waste timber from the slot with a 3/16" (5mm) chisel until it is the required size. (See photo # 6).

WARNING: From here on insert a tight fitting piece of scrap wood in the truss rod slot when clamping the neck in a vise. Failure to do so may result in a split neck and unnecessary anguish.

Photo # 6

N. Glue the peghead veneers to the peghead in a sandwich with the thick rosewood veneer on the outside. Use particle board scraps to protect the surfaces and distribute the clamping pressure. (See photo # 7).

O. When the glue has dried trim the excess veneer from the edges of the peghead with a chisel and sand flush with 80 grit sandpaper on a small block.

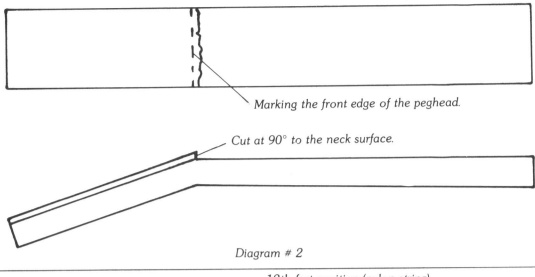

Marking the front edge of the peghead.

Cut at 90° to the neck surface.

Diagram # 2

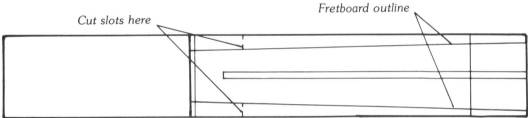

12th fret position (nylon string)
14th fret position (steel string)

Front edge of the nut.

Cut slots here

Fretboard outline

Diagram # 3

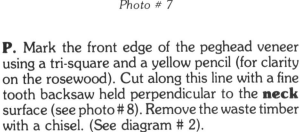

Photo # 7

Photo # 8

P. Mark the front edge of the peghead veneer using a tri-square and a yellow pencil (for clarity on the rosewood). Cut along this line with a fine tooth backsaw held perpendicular to the **neck** surface (see photo # 8). Remove the waste timber with a chisel. (See diagram # 2).

Q. Mark a line on the surface of the neck 3/16" (5mm) in front of and parallel to the edge of the peghead veneers. This will be the front edge of the nut. Mark the position of the 12th fret with a line drawn at 90° to the edge of the neck blank. (See diagram # 3).

R. Mark the outline of the fretboard using the appropriate template and make a saw cut into this line, on each side of the blank, about 3" (75mm) from the nut. (See diagram # 3 and photo # 9).

Photo # 9

S. Draw a centre line on the face of the peghead veneer and mark the outline of the peghead using a cardboard template (a yellow pencil is better for clarity).

T. Rough out the basic shape of the peghead with a coping saw (or bandsaw if available) and trim to its dimensions with a chisel (see photo # 10). Final sand with 80 grit sandpaper on a small sanding block making sure that the edges of the peghead are perpendicular to its face.

Photo # 10

U. For a steel string guitar mark and drill the machine head holes to accomodate the type of machine heads used. a spur or dowelling bit gives a much cleaner cut with minimal tearout.

Ua. For a classic guitar, mark the position of the holes for the plastic rollers on the side of the peghead. (Centering these holes is important so make sure to mark them accurately using the set of machine heads you intend to use as a guide).(See photo # 11). Drill these holes in a drill press for greater accuracy.

NOTE: Misalignment of these holes will cause the rollers to jam and, as a result be difficult to operate.

Photo # 11

Ub. Mark the position of the string slots on the face of the peghead. Use a ½" (12.5mm) spur bit to form the rounded ends of the slots. Use a coping saw to rough out the rest of the slots (see photo # 12). Then carefully sand the sides of the slots flat using 80 grit sandpaper.

Photo # 12

Uc. Fashion the string ramps using a piece of 80 grit sandpaper on a dowel stick (see photo # 13).

V. Mark the neck/body join as follows.

    a. For a steel string guitar mark the 14th fret position with a line at 90⁰ to the edge of the neck.

    b. For a classic guitar use the 12th fret position.

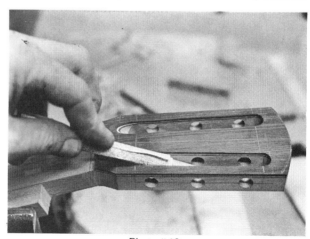

Photo # 13

W. True one of the 3″ X 6″ (75 X 150mm) surfaces of the heel block and clamp in position,without glue,so that its centre is approximately aligned with the neck/body join mark. When satisfied,dismantle,apply glue and clamp in position. (See # 14).

NOTE: Use a piece of scrap wood to protect the true surface of the neck. Check the position of the neck carefully when glueing as the glue will cause it to slip.

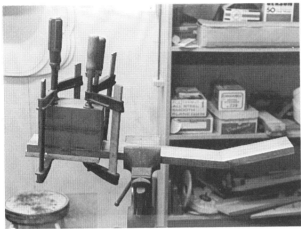
Photo # 14

X. When the glue is dry, at least one side of the heel block should be flush with the edge of the neck and at 90° to its surface. This can be accomplished with a block plane followed by sanding with a medium sanding block and 80 grit sandpaper. This step is critical to the symmetry of the instrument as the heel measurements are taken from this surface. The other side should also be trued if it overhangs the neck blank.

Y. Mark a line in the position of the neck/body join, on both sides of the heel block, at 90° to the fretboard surface of the neck blank. Using this line, position the heel/spanish foot template and mark its outline (see photo # 15).

Photo # 15

Z. For this step a bandsaw with a ¼″ (6.35mm) blade is very useful although it is readily accomplished with a coping saw used carefully.

Cut right on the line for the spanish foot,keeping in mind that the smoother the cut the less sanding will be required.

Cut the heel outline right on the line except where the block meets the neck blank. A ledge of approximately ⅛″ (3mm) should be left here to provide a safety margin when final shaping the neck. (See photo # 16).

Cut the depth of the spanish of the heel/spanish foot about ⅛″ (3mm) outside the line also as a safety margin.

Photo # 16

NOTE: Before moving on to the next stage it will be necessary to thickness and bend the sides.

AA. Mark the centre line of the bottom of the heel block and the position of the neck body join at 90° to it. Make a mark on this line ¼″ (6.35mm) each side of the centre line. Make similar marks on the fretboard surface of the neck blank. The purpose of these marks is guage the depth of the slots to be cut for the sides.

AB. Using a saw square as a guide,make the first cut for the side slots,with a tenon saw. (A piece of wood can be fashioned to serve the purpose of the saw square and clamped in place so that it guides the saw blade to cut perpendicular to the heel block (see photo # 17). Cut down to the marks made in the previous step. The width of the slots will need to be increased so that the sides fit neatly but not overtight. This can be achieved by taping a thin cabinet scraper to one side of the saw blade and recutting the slots as many times as necessary (See photo # 18). A piece of 80 grit sandpaper folded around a cabinet scraper is an effective,though slower,method of achieving this.

NOTE: The two sides should be aligned so take great care when widening the slots.

AC. Make a saw cut on each side of the neck approximately 4″ (100mm) from the side slots and in to the outline of the fretboard. This is to assist the carving of the heel.

Photo # 17

Photo # 18

AD. Fit the heel template into the side slots and tape securely in position. It will help to add posterboard shims to prevent it moving about.

AE. Mark the shape of the heel on the bottom of the heel block using a template. Mark the centre line of the heel curve using a piece of flexible plastic as a guide. This line will act as a guide when carving the heel. (See photo # 19).

Photo # 19

AF. Using a 1″ (25mm) chisel and a wooden mallet, roughly carve the *profile* of the heel. Final shape the profile with great care using only hand pressure on the chisel and working to the outer line first. The shape should be smooth and fairly symmetrical when viewed from the peghead (see photo # 20).

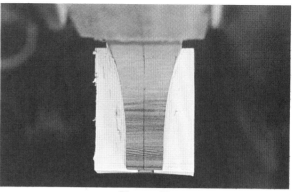

Photo # 20

AG. Shape the heel with a 1″ (25mm) chisel using hand pressure only and working in three facets either side (a bent chisel is handy where the curve of the heel meets the neck proper). When the three facets are cut, level the high spots and sand smooth with 120 grit sandpaper. (See photo # 21).

Photo # 21

AH. Mark the base of the spanish foot so that it is 2″ (50mm) wide (1″ each side of the centre line) and leave the top a full 3″ (75mm) wide. Trim the spanish foot to these marks using a block plane and sand smooth with 80 grit sandpaper on the medium sanding block. Smooth the inside curve of the spanish foot and round its edges (see photo # 22). Remember that this is visible through the soundhole.

The neck is now ready to move on to the assembly stage. Final shaping is left until the guitar is assembled and the fretboard glued in position.

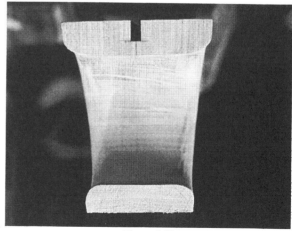

Photo # 22

The Sides

The Sides:

The timber for the sides should always match the back, not just in species but also as much as possible, in colouring and grain structure.

A. Each side should be thicknessed to 0.085" (2.3mm) using a smoothing plane then 80 grit sandpaper on a large sanding block. Clamp one end and work the other alternating, on both sides, until the desired thickness is reached (see photo # 1). Measure with the thickness guage and mark the readings with pencil as with the soundboard.

NOTE: Grain tearout is a fact of life when planing hardwoods so proceed carefully using a very sharp plane set for fine cuts. Waxing the sole of the plane will assist smooth operation.

Photo # 1

B. Place the two sides together with the grain bookmatched and mark the outside of each for identification. Mark the centre of the waist curve with a line at 90⁰ to one edge. For a classic guitar the waist curve is measured at 19" (485mm) from the *butt* end of the sides. For a dreadnaught steel string guitar the measurement is 20" (510mm).

C. The sides can now be bent using either a copper pipe heated with a butane torch (see photo # 2), or the side bending jig described in the jigs and tools section. For a more consistent result I feel it is better to take the time to construct a side bending jig. When using the jig it is still necessary to carry out final shaping on the hot copper pipe.

Photo # 2

Ca. If using the side bending jig tape the bindings to the edges of the sides (see photo # 3).

Photo # 3

Cb. Moisten the inner and outer surfaces of one side with a hand plant spray and sandwich between the stainless steel sheets with the surface you have chosen as the outer surface upward. Lightly clamp each end of the sandwich with spring clamps. Position this in the jig so that the tape at the waist curve is visible through the slot for the waist support bar.

Cc. Feed the waist support bar through and fix the springs in position. Wind the handle down so that the stainless steel/side sandwich is held between the waist block and the waist support bar (make sure that the side doesn't twist). Keep winding until the stainless steel begins to contact the upper and lower bouts of the body form, making sure that the stainless steel sandwich is correctly aligned in the jig. (See photo # 4). Switch on the lamps and leave for around ten minutes before proceeding.

Photo #4

Cd. Remove the spring clamps at each end and slowly wind down the waist block until it fits neatly into the waist curve of the body form with the stainless steel sandwich in place.

Ce. Position the lower bout clamping block near the waist block, attach its springs and slowly pull the block around to the bottom of the bending form.

Cf. Repeat this process for the upper bout. Leave the lamps on for about 45 minutes, switch off and allow to cool at least six hours before removing the side from the jig. The removal of the side is the reverse of its assembly sequence.

Cg. The side will be subject to a certain amount of springback and it will need to be touched up on a hot copper pipe to obtain a completely true shape.

NOTE: When using the hot copper pipe for the whole bending operation the sides and bindings will have to bent separately.

Da. Clamp the copper pipe firmly in a vise and position the flame of the butane torch just inside its mouth. Allow a few minutes for the pipe to heat.

Db. Lightly wet the side with a plant hand spray and, with the inside surface of the side facing up, begin to bend the waist by applying moderate hand pressure with the palm of the hands held about 3″ each side of the centre of the bend. Rock the side gently back and forth to avoid charring and check progress frequently on the side curve template. (See photo # 5).

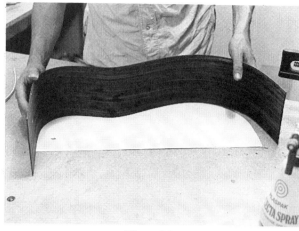

Photo # 5

NOTE: This is a tricky operation and the bending of the sides could take two days so proceed with care, keeping the wood moist and resisting the temptation to apply too much hand pressure and risk cracking the wood. To avoid cracking the wood along the grain when bending near the ends, place a piece of scrap wood under the palm of the relevant hand to distribute the pressure more evenly.

Dc. When the waist curve is complete, turn the side over and bend the upper and lower bouts working from the waist curve toward the ends. It is best to work slowly and check progress, with the template, frequently.

Dd. The bindings can be shaped in much the same manner as the sides using the fingertips to apply pressure.

Any slight variation in shape can be rectified when assembling on the workboard.

When the sides are complete it is worthwhile sanding any scorch or water marks, from the inside, with 80 grit sandpaper.

28

The Back

The Back:

Joining:

A. Place the two halves of the back side by side in the bookmatched position and decide which edges are to be joined. If the grain is curved it is a rule of thumb that the grain should converge toward the upper bout (see diagram # 1).

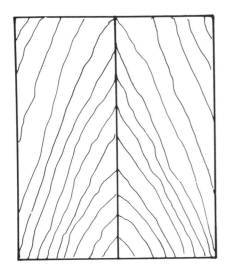

Diagram # 1

B. The centre join of the back is executed in the same manner as the centre join of the soundboard. However, if using a resinous species such as rosewood, wipe the edges of the join with a paper towel soaked in acetone before glueing. This procedure is worth making a habit of, with rosewood, as it will greatly improve the effectiveness of the glue.

Thicknessing:

C. This procedure is also the same as for thicknessing the soundboard except that it usually more difficult do to the nature of hardwoods. Don't rush this step or you will experience a lot of problems with grain tearout. The thickness of the back should be 0.125" (3mm) and it is best to sand with 80 grit sandpaper on a large sanding block.

Inlaying the Centre Back Strip:

The back strip is basically a decorative piece of wood inlayed over the centre join. I have a preference for matching the back strip to the bindings although a selection of wood marquetry strips are sold for this purpose.

Cutting the Groove With a Router:

NOTE: When cutting the back strip groove with a router remember to wear eye protection!

D. Clamp the back to the square workboard and set up a straight fence using a length of aluminium 1½" X ¼" (38 X 6.35mm) about 24" (600mm) long. This fence should be clamped in position so that the router bit will cut along the centre join.

E. Use a router bit slightly smaller than the width of the back strip and set up to cut a slot half the thickness of the back in depth. Make short test cuts at each end to check depth and alignment.

F. Cut the groove by making a pass along the back with the router base firmly held against the aluminium fence. Be careful not to rotate the router base. (See photo # 1).

Photo # 1

G. To widen the slot, simply apply strips of masking tape to the router base where it contacts the fence, making sure the tape doesn't go under the base. Apply as many pieces of tape as is necessary to widen the groove and provide a snug fit for the backstrip.

Cutting the Groove by Hand:

H. Measure the width of the back strip and halve it, then, using the centre join of the back as a reference point, use this measurement to mark the location of the backstrip. It is only necessary to mark each end of the slot. Check the width of the slot with the backstrip and mark with a sharp knife at each end.

I. Set up a metal straight edge along one set of marks and clamp tightly in position. Make sure that it is set up so that any slip of the knife cuts into the waste area. Using a very sharp knife make several deep cuts using the straight edge as a guide. Repeat this for the other side of the slot.

J. Remove the straight edge and chisel out the slot to about half the thickness of the back.

Fitting the Backstrip:

K. If using a rosewood back or a rosewood backstrip, leach with acetone.

L. Run enough glue in the slot to thinly cover all surfaces, press the backstrip into position and clamp. Use a length of 2" X 1" (50 X 25mm) with a waxed edge to distribute the clamping pressure. (See photo # 2).

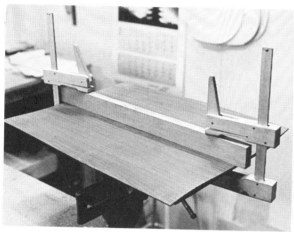

Photo # 2

M. When the glue has dried the backstrip can be levelled to the surface of the back using a cabinet scraper and then 80 grit sandpaper on the large sanding block (see photo # 3).

Photo # 3

N. Mark the body shape on the outside of the back and cut out, leaving about ⅛ (3mm) outside the line. A bandsaw or coping saw, used carefully, are best for this operation. Leave a protrusion about ½" X ½" (12 X 12mm) at the heel end to assist in locating the back when glueing.

NOTE: If using rosewood for the back, mark the shape with a yellow pencil.

O. Using a piece of soundboard off-cut make the marriage strip with the grain orientation as shown in diagram # 2. The dimensions should be around 1" X 17" (25 X 425mm). The function of the marriage strip is to strengthen the centre join.

Profile

Diagram # 2

P. Before glueing the marriage strip in place mark its position with a length of masking tape about ½" (12.5mm) each side of the centre join. The purpose of this is to prevent the marriage strip from slipping when glue s applied.

Q. Glue the marriage strip in place using GO sticks. Protect the surface and distribute the pressure with scrap timber about ½" (12.5mm) wide. If using a rosewood back, leach with acetone first. After glueing, wipe away excess glue.

R. When dry, shape the marriage strip so that its profile is a low curve (see diagram # 2). Use a 1" (25mm) chisel and a small sanding block with 120 grit sandpaper for this purpose (see photo # 4). Remove the masking tape and clean up the excess glue.

Photo # 4

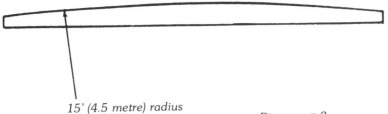

15' (4.5 metre) radius

Diagram # 3

Making the Back Braces:

The back braces can be made from spruce, cedar or mahogany ½" (12.5mm) high and ⅜" wide, preferably with vertical grain. They have a curved glueing surface of 15 feet (4.5 metres) radius. This is to effect the back curve which is necessary for strength. (See diagram # 3). Each piece will need to be around 16" (400mm) long.

S. Make a cardboard template of the back curve from the diagrams in the back of the book.

T. The curve on the back braces is best effected by curving all four at once. Lightly glue all four braces together with a spot of glue at each end and one near the centre. Mark the centre of the braces on the upper surface (the one not being curved) with a pencil line across all four. This is to assist in aligning the braces when glueing to the back.

U. Using the template, draw a curve on each side of the group of braces with a sharp pencil and, holding the braces in a vise, carefully shape to the line using a block plane then 80 grit sandpaper on a small block. (See photo # 5).

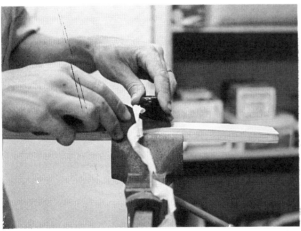

Photo # 5

V. Once the curve is effected gently separate the braces using a razor blade or scalpel.

W. Mark the position of the braces on the marriage strip using the following formula. The upper bout brace is in the same relative position as the upper bout brace on the soundboard; the next is 4½" (113mm) from it and the remaining two are located by dividing the remaining distance by three.

X. Each brace should, in turn, be placed in its position using a set square to ensure that they are at 90° to the marriage strip. Mark the marriage strip with a pencil on each side of each brace and also mark the back near its edges to assist in aligning the braces when glueing. (See photo # 6).

Photo # 6

Y. Cut out the section of the marriage strip where each brace crosses using a sharp knife to define the edges of the cutout and a narrow chisel to remove the wood. Also remove all the marriage strip above the brace on the upper bout.

Z. Glue the back braces, two at a time, using GO sticks. Make sure to use the posterboard protector between the back and the GO stick board. To effect the curve it will be necessary to build ramps with strips of posterboard about 1" (25mm) wide (see diagram # 4). Use Titebond and clean up excess glue before it dries.

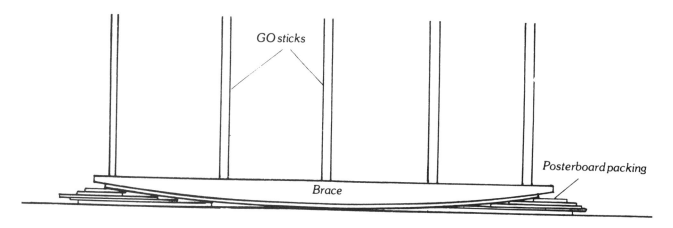

GO sticks

Posterboard packing

Brace

Diagram # 4

Za. When all braces are glued and dry, cut to length so that they overhang the sides about ⅛" (3mm). Round the top edge and scallop about 2" (50mm) in from each end leaving about   " (1.5mm) at the end. (See photo # 7).
The back is now ready for assembly.

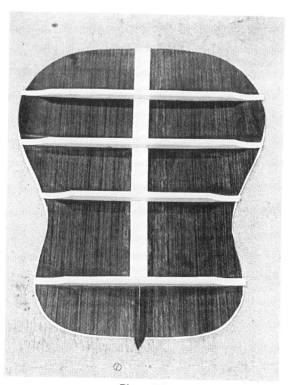

Photo # 7

Assembly

Assembly:

When the basic components of the guitar (i.e. the soundboard, neck, sides and back) are complete they should be assembled, as the measurements for the fretboard, binding, bridge etc. are taken from this basic assembly.

Neck to Body:

A. The upper section of the spanish foot has to be rebated to accomodate the soundboard. The outside surface of the soundboard and the upper (fretboard) surface of the neck should be in the same plane. The depth of the rebate is measured by marking, with a sharp pencil, the thickness of the upper (veneered) section of the soundboard around the upper section of the spanish foot (see photo # 1).

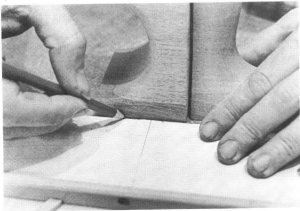

Photo # 1

B. Chisel then sand the rebate to its correct depth using a 1″ (25mm) chisel and a small sanding block with 80 grit sandpaper. Check progress frequently with a 12″ (300mm) rule to ensure that the neck and soundboard remain in the same plane. A good fit is essential so, if too much wood is removed, build up with suitable veneers, allow to dry, and sand again. (See photos # 2 & 3).

Photo # 2

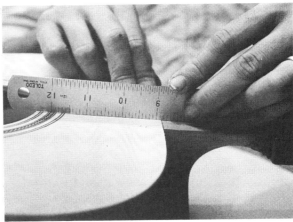

Photo # 3

C. Mount the guitar shaped workboard in a bench top vise, preferably one that rotates (a side mounting woodworking vise is unsuitable). Cut out a section of the posterboard protector to allow access to the tee nut hole and place the protector in position.

D. Make two ″ (5mm) pins and insert them into the holes in the neck section of the workboard so that they protrude about ¼″ (6.35mm). For a steel string guitar these pins will need to be wrapped with masking tape to ensure a snug fit in the truss rod slot. For a classic guitar two holes ¼″ (6.35mm) deep will have to be drilled, on the centreline of the neck, to correspond with the holes in the workboard.

E. A posterboard protector of the same thickness as that for the guitar body should be made for the neck. It will be approximately 12″ X 3″ (300 X 75mm) with two holes cut out for the neck locating pins. This is placed on the workboard (see photo # 4).

F. Make a soundhole clamp from ½″ (12.5mm) plywood or particle board.

Photo # 4

G. Sand the upper bout of the soundboard to its final shape.

H. As the soundboard is going to be face down, mark its centre at each end of the inside with a sharp pencil. Place the soundboard face down on the workboard (using the protector) and align so that the centrelines of each coincide. Clamp firmly in position with the soundhole clamp.

I. Position the neck,dry,so that the neck slot is located by the two pins and the ledge of the spanish foot is in position over the soundboard.

NOTE: The neck/body join is critical to the symmetry of the finished instrument,so check the alignment carefully.

J. When satisfied, remove the neck, apply glue to the ledge on the spanish foot, reposition and clamp with a large metal sash cramp and clean up the excess glue. Clamp the neck to the workboard using a piece of scrap wood to protect its surface. This clamp will stay in place until assembly is complete. (See photo # 5).

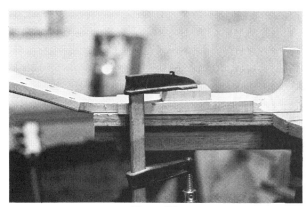

Photo # 5

Fitting the Sides:

K. Mark the length of the sides at the neck by placing each side,in turn,on the body template and drawing a perpendicular line at least ¼" (6.35mm) short of the centre line. Cut to this line with a fine tooth dovetail saw.

L. Sand the inside and outside of the sides smooth for about 3" (75mm) along their length until they fit their respective slots in the neck neatly,but not tightly. Fit the sides into the neck and check their length. If necessary cut to fit.

M. Locate the sides in the neck slot,without glue,and clamp in position with dowel clamps and cam clamps using the pencil outline on the soundboard as a guide,not the bandsawn shape. As the edges of the sides may not be level mark a line parallel to the soundboard using a compass (see photo # 6).

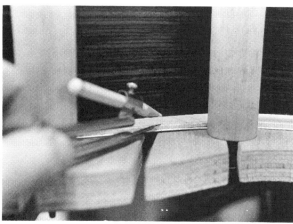

Photo # 6

N. Remove the sides and trim roughly to the line with a chisel used carefully.

O. Apply glue to the INSIDE surface of the side only,and only sufficient to cover the spanish foot area. (Leach with acetone if using rosewood). Fit the sides into the slot and make sure that they stand vertical.

NOTE: The reason that glue is applied only to the inside surfaces is that excess glue is difficult to remove from the heel area. This side/neck join is not structural and in traditional spanish construction is not glued at all.

P. Clamp the sides into shape and,where they overlap,draw a line perpendicular to the centre line of the workboard. Clamp the end of each side to dowel clamps using scrap wood on the inside to distribute the clamping pressure and minimise the risk of splitting the sides. Cut to the line using a coping saw or a hacksaw blade held in the hand. (See photo # 7).

Photo # 7

Q. Make the end block from ½" (12.5mm) plywood 2" (50mm) wide and longer than the depth of the butt,to allow for trimming. One end should be square both ways and the inner (non-glued) surface rounded and smooth.

R. Make a butt glueing support block from a piece of solid timber 2" X 2" X 5" (50 X 50 X 125mm) also with one end square both ways (see diagram # 1).

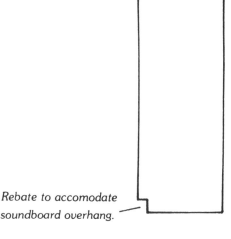

Rebate to accomodate soundboard overhang.

Diagram # 1

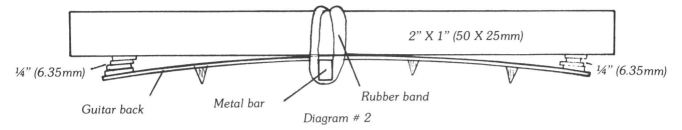

¼" (6.35mm)   2" X 1" (50 X 25mm)   ¼" (6.35mm)

Guitar back   Metal bar   Rubber band

Diagram # 2

S. Wax the appropriate surface of the butt glueing block and clamp in position so that its surface is square to the *centre* of the soundboard. Use a setsquare to check this alignment (see photo # 8).

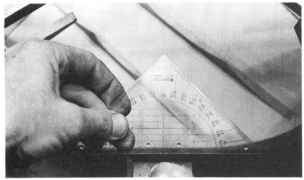

Photo # 8

T. Using a thin piece of scrap wood to protect the surface, clamp the end block in position using two deep throat G cramps and two standard G cramps. When satisfied with the alignment, dismantle and apply glue to the end block both on the large surface and the end that contacts the soundboard. Clamp in position making sure that the end block contacts the soundboard and that no large gap exists between the side and the soundboard. Clean up excess glue.

U. The sides are glued to soundboard with little blocks of spruce, western red cedar or mahogany called *tentallones*. These are made by cutting up strips of kerfed lining into individual segments and cleaning up the rough edges with a file.

V. The tentallones are glued in place, around the sides, one at a time, by putting a smear of glue on their two glueing surfaces and placing in position with your fingertips. There is no need to clamp. (See photo # 9).

NOTE: Allow the tentallones plenty of time to dry as there is often a lot of tension if the sides were forced into shape when clamping. Remove the clamps, holding the sides in shape, when dry.

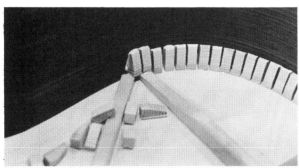

Photo # 9

W. Set up the lengthwise curve of the back by the following method. Place a length of 2" X 1" (50 X 50mm), on edge, along the back strip then place a metal bar at least ⅜" (9.5mm) thick underneath, behind the second brace (i.e. near the middle). Loop a large rubber band over one end of the metal bar, back over the 2" X 1" and then hook over the other end of the metal bar. Place ¼" (6.35mm) of packing between the 2" X 1" and the back at each end of the back. If the middle of the 2" X 1" no longer contacts the back, increase the tension on the rubber bands. (See diagram # 2).

X. Take the four threaded rod, nut and washer sets and position them on the workboard so that they are at approximately the widest points of the upper and lower bouts and as close to the sides as possible. Firmly clamp the threaded rod to the workboard with the wing nuts and then lightly clamp the back into the upper nut and washer set with the back curve jig still attached.

Y. The back should be in position so that its distance from the workboard is the same at each side of the upper bout and the same at each side of the lower bout (the height need not be the same for the upper and lower bouts). The distance that the back is above the sides is incidental but is is important that the *difference* between the height of the back above the workboard at the heel end and the butt end is the same as the *difference* between the actual measurments for the depth of the heel and the butt. This measurement is vital to the symmetry of the instrument.

Z. Mark the depth of the body at the butt and the depth of the body at the heel and, using a compass, mark a line around the sides parallel to the inside surface of the back. Start at the butt and work toward the heel. If the line doesn't coincide with both the butt and heel depth marks check all measurement before proceeding. (See photo # 10)

Photo # 10

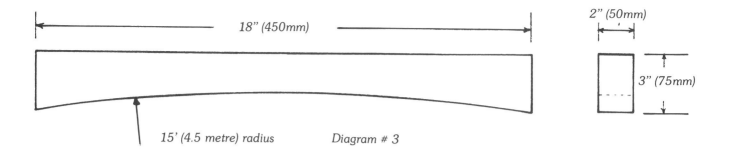

18" (450mm)   2" (50mm)

3" (75mm)

15' (4.5 metre) radius   Diagram # 3

AA. Remove the back and dismantle the back curve jig. Remove the threaded rods and trim the excess wood from the sides down to the line using a chisel. It is most important that the sides be held firmly during this operation to prevent splitting.

AB. The kerfed lining for the back can now be glued in position using wooden clothes pegs,strengthened with small rubber bands,as spring clamps. The kerfed lining will need to be cut into suitable lengths to compensate for the curve of the sides and should protrude about   " (2mm) above the sides. (See photo # 11).

Photo # 11

AC. Using the posterboard template of the back curve make a concave sanding block from a piece of 3" X 2" (75 X 50mm) about 18" (450mm) in length. The concave surface should be covered with formica (for easy removal of worn sandpaper) and 80 grit sandpaper affixed with rubber cement. (See diagram # 3).

AD. Using the curved sanding block,sand the kerfed lining down to the level of the sides using a lengthwise motion. Trim the spanish foot to its approximate thickness a block plane before sanding. The end block should also be roughly trimmed,with a chisel. Great care should be exercised to prevent the sides from flexing. To do this,simply place a number of dowel clamps against the sides in various positions. (See photo # 12).

Fitting the Back:

AE. Remove the soundhole clamp and hold the
AE. REMOVE THE SOUNDHOLE CLAMP and hold the body in place with a ½" (12.5mm) high dowel clamp placed at either side of the lower bout.

Photo # 12

AF. Place the back in its approximate position and,if necessary,cut the excess length from the spanish foot to give clearance to the upper bout back brace. Also trim the marriage strip at the butt to give clearance to the end block.

AG. Locate the back in its correct position and mark the sides where the braces overlap (see photo # 13). Remove the back and,using a fine tooth backsaw and a chisel,make a series of knotches in the sides and kerfed lining to accomodate the back braces.

NOTE: Don't cut these too deep as they need to be covered by the bindings.

Photo # 13

AH. Replace the back in its correct position and hold in place with a large (size 108) rubber band. Drill a 1/16 (1.5mm) hole through the protrusion at the heel end,insert a small brad (hardboard nail) and tap it gently into the heel about ⅛" (3mm). The purpose of this nail is to locate the back positively when glueing.

AI. When satisfied with the fit,remove the back,apply glue to the spanish foot,kerfed lining and end block,and replace the back using the small nail as a guide. Hold the back in position with large rubber bands and,cam clamps at the spanish foot and end block. (See photo # 14).

NOTE: Two or more rubber bands can be linked for increased length.

AJ. When the back has had sufficient drying time,remove the rubber bands and all the clamps and the guitar can be removed from the soundboard. Don't disturb the workboard or protectors as they will be required when cutting the binding channels.

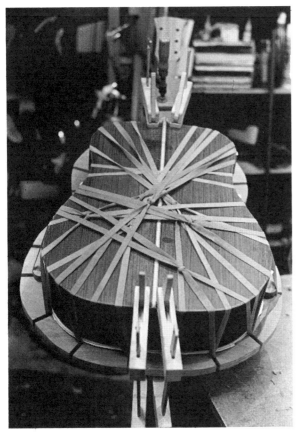

Photo # 14

Notes:

Binding
and Purfling

Binding and Purfling:

NOTE: This step should be undertaken after the basic assembly is complete.

A. Hold the guitar securely, on its side, on the benchand carefully trim the overhanging edges with a chisel. The sides should then be sanded flat using a medium sanding block with 80 grit sandpaper other than near the heel where only 120 grit should be used.

NOTE: It is important that the sides be sanded flat before fitting as any excessive future sanding will lead to variations in their thickness.

B. Fit a ⅜" (10mm) bit in the router, remove the base plate and fit the binding/purfling channel jig. Adjust the bit so that it cuts a channel which will allow the binding to sit just proud of the sides and back. Make test cuts on a piece of scrap timber and check with a piece of binding until satisfied with the fit. If using the router is a frightening proposition build up your confidence by working on scrap bits of wood. Almost all my students were deterred by this step yet no disasters occured.

NOTE: Please wear a full face shield or, at the very least, safety goggles when using the router. These tools revolve at speeds in excess of 20,000 r.p.m. but are quite safe if treated with care and respect.

C. Mount the guitar, soundboard down, on the workboard with protectors in place as when glueing on the back. Clamp the neck and hold the lower bout steady with two low dowel clamps (they must be low enough for the jig handle to pass over).

D. Place the router on the back near the heel so that the bit is well away from the side. Hold the hand grip of the jig firmly in the right hand and tilt back slightly so that when routing commences the lower ball bearing contacts the side first (see photo # 1).

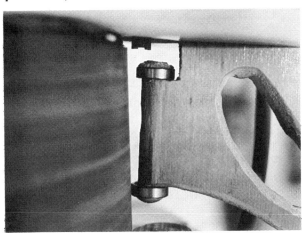

Photo # 1

E. Start the router and carefully slide the jig in to the work using right hand pressure. When the lower ball bearing makes contact keep pushing until the upper ball bearing makes contact by which time the bit will be cutting the channel. (See photo # 2). Move the jig around to the butt and then back to the heel to ensure a clean even cut.

Photo # 2

NOTE: The success of this procedure depends on the following;
1. Firm, not hard, right hand pressure on the jig handle to keep both ball bearings in contact with the side.
2. The handle of the jig must remain perpendicular to a tangent of the side curve at all points (see diagram # 1).
3. The left hand should only be used to lightly guide the router on its path. Excessive left hand pressure will cause the router to rock and cut a channel of varying depth.

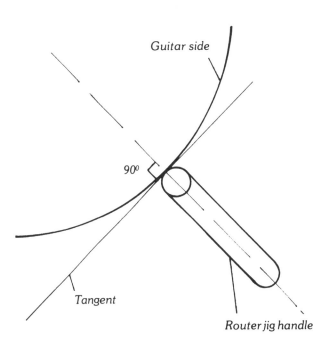

Diagram # 1

F. Repeat the procedure for the other side and clean up any ragged edges with a small smooth file.

NOTE: The router will not cut the channel right up to the heel. This will have to be done carefully by hand, using a sharp knife and chisel.

G. Scribe a line between the ends of the routed channel using a sharp knife with a cabinet scraper as a guide. This line should be cut several times to make it as deep as possible. (See photo # 3).

Photo # 3

H. Trim down to the depth of the knife cut with a small chisel then deepen the knife cut again. Repeat this procedure until the channel matches the routed channel in depth and width. The heel will need to be trimmed at the same time to accomodate the heel cap which is the same depth as the binding.

I. Tape the binding in place, on one side, using masking tape, at various points. Check to ensure a neat fit and mark to length at each end using the centre of the back strip as a guide. Remove the binding and cut to length with a fine backsaw.

J. Repeat this process for the other side.

K. Glue the bindings in place starting at the butt, using masking tape strips about 1" (25mm) apart to hold them. When each side is glued drive a small nail into the heel and force the ends of the binding into position with a waxed wooden wedge (see photo # 4). If the bindings are too long quickly trim them with a chisel without removing.

Photo # 4

L. If using herringbone purfling on a steel string guitar, soak the herringbone in very hot water for ten to fifteen minutes (use a bath or laundry tub for length). Split the herringbone along its length to about 3" (75mm) from the end.

NOTE:
1. Split in the direction of the arrow (see diagram # 2).
2. Use a dull knife.
3. Stay on the same side of the centre white strip.
4. Tape each piece of herringbone to the bending form so that it adapts to its required shape.
5. Do not allow to dry completely before using.

Split in this direction

Diagram # 2

M. When the bindings on the back are dry, remove the masking tape, turn the guitar over and mount on workboard with the soundboard facing up. Clamp the neck using a block of wood as a levelling spacer and another block of wood to protect the glueing surface of the fretboard (see photo # 5). Wedges will be needed to support the back due to its arching (see diagram # 3). Dowel clamps will be needed to steady the lower bout.

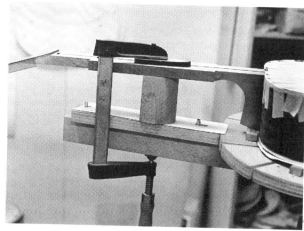

Photo # 5

N. The binding channel can be routed in much the same manner as the back. However, the bindings need only indent about ½" (12.5mm) beyond the edge of the neck.

O. Another channel will have to be cut for the purfling whether you are using herringbone or black/white strips. The router jig will have to be adjusted to allow for both the extra width and more shallow depth (no more than the thickness of the soundboard) of the purfling. Use the same piece of scrap timber that was used to test the binding channel to guage the extra width required for the purfling channel.

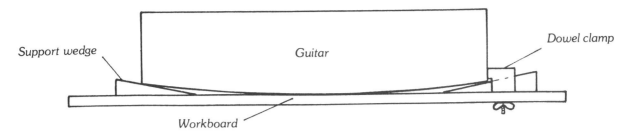

Support wedge   Guitar   Dowel clamp

Workboard

Diagram # 3

NOTE: *It is advisable to lightly sand the furry edges of the binding channel before cutting the purfling channel.*

P. Route the purfling channel using the same method as for the binding channel.

Q. Tape the purflings and bindings in place temporarily, mark their length, then remove and cut to length. Keep in mind that there is some leeway at the neck as the fretboard will cover this.

R. Working one side at a time and starting at the butt, glue both purflings and bindings in place using masking tape strips about 1" (25mm) apart to hold in place. Make sure that there is glue between all surfaces, including each piece of purfling.

S. Remove the guitar from the workboard and hold against the bench with the butt facing up. Use a clamp each side and a double rubber band to hold it in place (see photo # 6). Be sure to protect the peghead with a block of foam rubber where it contacts the floor, also protect the soundboard where it contacts the bench.

Photo # 6

T. Lay a piece of masking tape over the centre line of the butt. Hold the butt strip in position, aligned with the centre back strip, and scribe a line each side with a sharp knife. Do not scribe the bindings.

NOTE: *The butt strip can be made from an off-cut of the centre back strip.*

U. Using the edge of a cabinet scraper as a guide, make several deep cuts along each line with a sharp knife then chisel to the required depth with a narrow chisel. (See photo # 7).

V. Cut the butt strip to length and glue in position. It should be a tight fit and not require clamping.

Photo # 7

W. Make the heel cap, from a piece of rosewood, to the rough shape of the heel. Sand one face, and the straight edge, flat.

Y. Ensure that the surface of the heel is flat, leach the heel cap with acetone, apply glue and clamp in place (see photo # 8).

Photo # 8

Z. When the glue is dry, trim the heel cap to shape with a chisel, then plane to thickness with a block plane so that its upper surface is a continuation of the line of the back. (See photo # 9).

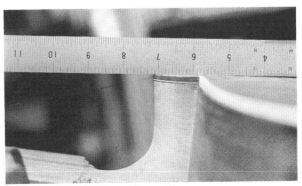

Photo # 9

Notes:

The Adjustable
Truss Rod

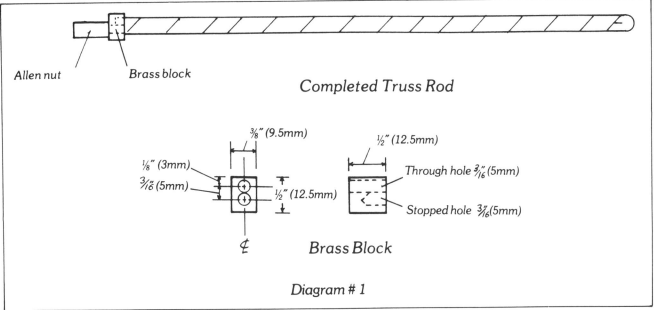

Allen nut   Brass block

Completed Truss Rod

⅜″ (9.5mm)

⅛″ (3mm)
³⁄₁₆″ (5mm)

½″ (12.5mm)

½″ (12.5mm)   Through hole ³⁄₁₆″ (5mm)

Stopped hole ³⁄₁₆″ (5mm)

₵   Brass Block

Diagram # 1

The Adjustable Truss Rod:

NOTE: *This does not apply to classic guitars.*
The purpose of the truss rod in a steel string guitar is to counteract the tension of the strings. An adjustable truss rod is useful to take into account such factors as climatic changes and variations in string tension for different string guages.
Diagram # 1 shows a completed truss rod.
A. Measure the distance from the peghead end of the truss rod slot to a point approximately 2″ (50mm) from the edge of the soundhole. Mark this distance on the ³⁄₁₆ steel rod by scratching with a file.
B. Using a butane gas torch, heat the rod to cherry red at this mark (see photo # 1).
C. Bend double and hammer flat at the point of bending.

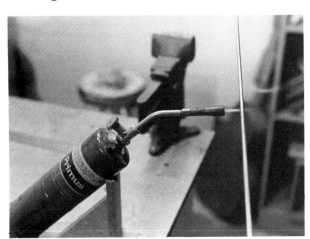

Photo # 1

D. Shape a block of brass to ½″ X ½″ X ⅜″ (12.5mm X 12.5mm X 9.5mm). Mark the position of the holes and punch the centres. (See diagram # 1).
E. Drill the two ³⁄₁₆″ holes, one through and one stopped (see diagram # 1).
F. Cut off the end of the double rod so that it stops 2¼″ (57mm) short of the soundhole. This is fitted to the *stopped* hole of the brass block.
G. Cut off the other end so that the rod protrudes no further than ¼″ (6.35mm) beyond the through hole of the block.
H. Remove the brass block and grip the rod tightly in a vise. Thread the long end of the rod down to the length of the short rod using a ³⁄₁₆″ 32 threads per inch stock and die set (see photo # 2).

Photo # 2

NOTE: *The thread has to match that of the allen nut. If no allen nut is available, use a conventional hexagon nut and cut a suitable thread on the rod.*

I. Replace the brass block, screw on the allen nut, grip the brass block in a vise and wrap ½″ (12.5mm) fibreglass reinforced packaging tape tightly around both rods in a spiral. Take care to wrap the tape neatly and not overlap as this will make it difficult to fit in the truss rod slot.

Notes:

The Fretboard

The Fretboard:

A. With the fretboard blank set up on the flat shooting board plane one surface approximately flat using a smoothing plane (see photo # 1).

NOTE: 1. The plane will need to be very sharp.
2. Both ebony and rosewood can be tough woods to plane as they often have cranky grain (i.e. the direction of the grain changes in the length of the board).

Photo # 1

B. Check with a straight edge and sand level using the large sanding block and 80 grit sandpaper.
C. Using a marking guage set at ¼" (6.35mm), mark the thickness of the fretboard on each edge of the blank.
D. Working to these marks, repeat steps A & B.
E. True one edge of the board by holding it in a vise then planing and sanding with a large sanding block until perfectly straight and at 90° to the surface.
F. Sand one end of the board until it is at 90° to the true edge and at 90° to the surface. This will be the nut end of the fretboard and all fret spacing is measured from here. Check this with a tri-square. (See photo # 2).
G. Find the approximate centre of the board (it may vary in width) and, using a marking guage, lightly mark a line through this point parallel to the true edge.

Photo # 2

H. Using the cardboard template, mark each of the fret positions on this line with a sharp pointed bradawl and then mark the fret slot positions, in pencil, using the tri-square held against the true edge (see diagram # 1).
I. Mark a line on each edge of the fretboard to guage the depth of the fret slots using a marking guage set at ⅛" (3mm).
J. Clamp the fretboard to the bench so that the true edge overhangs about ¼" (6.35mm). Using a saw square, or similar guide, and a dovetail saw with the capacity to cut an accurate 0.025" (0.6mm) kerf, cut each fret slot to the required depth. (See photo # 3).

NOTE: A guide can be made by simply fixing two pieces of 2" X 1" (50 X 25mm) at precisely 90° to each other. The object of the exercise is to hold the saw blade vertical as well as at 90° to the edge.

Photo # 3

K. Using the posterboard template centred on the centre line of the slotted surface of fretboard, mark the outline of the fretboard preferably with yellow or white pencil (see diagram # 1).
L. Using either a bandsaw or coping saw, carefully cut away the excess wood about ˝ (1.5mm) outside the line. Plane and sand both edges straight and at 90° to the surface. It is important that the taper of the fretboard be even on both sides.

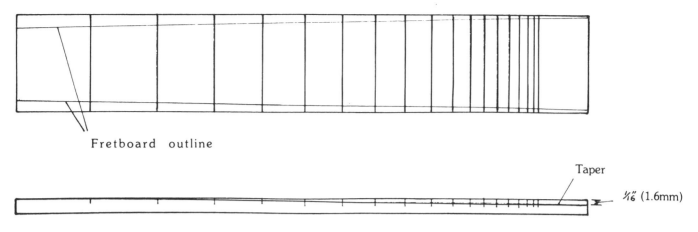

Fretboard outline

Taper

⅟₁₆″ (1.6mm)

Marking the bass side taper for a classic guitar.

Diagram # 1

M. For a classic guitar the fretboard is usually tapered in thickness on the bass side to compensate for the fact that the bass strings have a wider arc of vibration.

Ma. Hold the fretboard in a vise with the bass edge facing up. Mark a point ″ (1.5mm) down from the slotted surface at the 18th fret. Using a straight edge as a guide, draw a line to pass through this point to the slotted edge of the nut end of the fretboard (see diagram # 1).

Mb. Using the flat shooting board, plane the bass side of the fretboard down to the line tapering gently to the treble side at the soundhole end.

NOTE: If the grain of fretboard is cranky it is worthwhile simply sanding this taper with 80 grit sandpaper on the large sanding block, a longer, but less nerve wracking prospect.

N. For a steel string guitar the fretted surface is usually curved to facilitate ease of playing for most playing styles.

Na. Mark a line on each edge ⅟₁₆ (1.5mm) down from the slotted surface, using a marking guage.

Nb. Using the flat shooting board and a smoothing plane, plane the profile of the fretboard into several facets taking care to leave the centre line intact as a reference point (see diagram # 2).

2 Facets

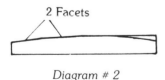

Diagram # 2

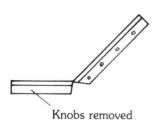

Knobs removed

Diagram # 3

Nc. Sand a smooth curve using 80 grit sandpaper on the large sanding block. Gradually work through 120 and 180 up to 320 grit.

O. The fret slots should now be cleaned and deepened, if necessary, with the 0.025″ (0.6mm) dovetail saw. Use an offcut of fretwire to check the depth of the slots (see diagram # 3).

P. The fretboard should now be clamped dry in its position on the neck and the curve of the soundhole marked on it. The soundhole cutout works well for this (see photo # 4).

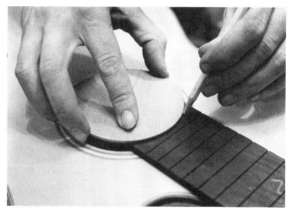

Photo # 4

Q. Cut off the excess fretboard and sand the edge of the curve smooth using 80 grit sandpaper on a large dowel, or something similar. Check that the curve of the fretboard matches the curve of the soundhole when correctly located.

R. Fret position markers should now be fitted to *steel string guitar* fretboards. These are usually fitted, both on the edge and the slotted surface of the fretboard, at fret numbers 3,5,7,9,12,15 & 17. Edge position markers can be made from fine white plastic knitting needles or brass or aluminium rod. Surface position markers come in a wonderful array of shapes and sizes; some quite simple and others of dubious aesthetic value. I recommend dots for a first guitar. Classic guitars are not usually fitted with position markers so the next few steps need not apply.

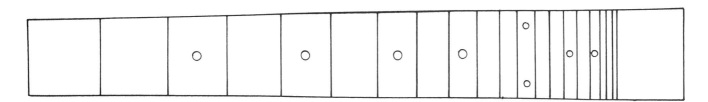

Diagram # 4

S. To locate the edge position markers, mark a line along the centre of the edge of the fretboard which will face the player. Mark their positions along this line (e.g. the 3rd fret position marker is located midway between the 2nd and 3rd fret slots and the 5th midway between the 4th and 5th fret slot, and so on). The exception is the 12th fret where two dots should be fitted (see diagram # 4).

T. Drill a slightly oversize hole, at each position, about ⅛" (3mm) deep.

U. The surface position markers are located in a similar manner (see diagram # 4).

V. Drill a slightly oversize hole for the surface position dots no deeper than the dot to be used.

W. Cut the edge position markers into ¼" (6.35mm) lengths.

X. Mix up a small amount of 5 minute epoxy and wood dust from the fretboard and glue all position markers in place. When thoroughly dry, sand smooth to the fretboard surface.

NOTE: The following applies to both classic and steel string guitars.

Y. To push in the frets, hardwood cauls should be made. The caul for a steel string guitar will need to be appropriately concave (see diagram # 5).

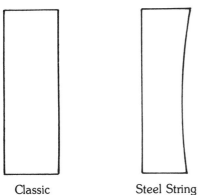

Classic   Steel String

Diagram # 5

Z. Cut the fretwire into lengths, with each length about ⅛" (3mm) longer than its appropriate slot. Use carpenters pincers.

AA. Run a bead of P.V.A. glue along each fret slot prior to fitting the fret. The purpose of this is not so much to glue the fret in place as to minimise chipping when refretting.

AB. Frets 1 and 11 are not fitted at this stage so the slots should be taped with masking tape to act as a reminder.

AC. Start at the 2nd fret and gently tap one end of the fret into place with a hammer. Then, using the hardwood caul, squeeze the fret into place in a vise with flat, deep jaws (an engineers vise is unsuitable). (See photo # 5). Frets can also be tapped in using a hammer with the fretboard laid flat on the bench. However, I feel this produces a less consistent result, especially when inexperienced.

Photo # 5

AD. As each fret is fitted wipe off excess glue with a damp cloth, then dry.

AE. When all frets (except 1 & 11) are fitted, place the fretboard (which will now be bent backward) in a vise, held between two lengths of wood with one edge protruding about ½" (12.5mm). The fret ends can now be filed flush with the edge of the fretboard (see photo # 6) and chamfered to 45° (see diagram # 6).

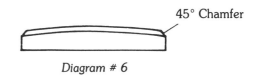

45° Chamfer

Diagram # 6

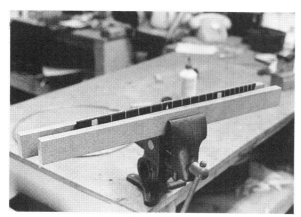

Photo # 6

AF. Place the fretboard clamping guide on the fretboard and, using a bradawl or sharp nail, mark the position of the guide holes at the 1st and 11th frets.

AG. Drill a small hole through the fret slot at each of these marks. The holes should be able to fit a small nail (brad) tightly.

AH. Tap a small nail into each of these holes until it just protrudes beyond the bottom of the fretboard. The purpose of these nails is to locate the fretboard securely when glueing.

AI. Clamp the fretboard in position and, with the neck well supported, tap the nails gently so that they leave an indentation in the surface of the neck (see photo # 7).

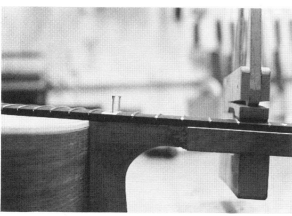

Photo # 7

AJ. Set up the fretboard clamping caul and clamp in position making sure to protect the under surface of the neck with scrap wood. Check the alignment of the fretboard.

AK. Dismantle the clamping jig, and remove the fretboard.

AL. For a steel string guitar, fit the truss rod at this point. It will be necessary to remove some wood from the soundboard to accommodate the brass block and adjusting nut. Ensure that the truss rod doesn't project above the surface of the neck or soundboard. The allen nut should sit *lowest* in the slot.

AM. Apply glue to the under surface of the fretboard and clamp in position. Check again for alignment. (See photo # 8).

AN. Leave at least two hours then remove the clamps and clamping guide.

AO. Remove the masking tape from the fret slots 1 and 11 and run a bead of P.V.A. glue in each slot. Support the neck in the appropriate places and gently tap the frets into place with a hammer. Wash off the excess glue.

NOTE: When hammering frets let the weight of the hammer head do the work, just let it fall from about 6" (150mm).

AP. Level the fret ends and chamfer.

Photo # 8

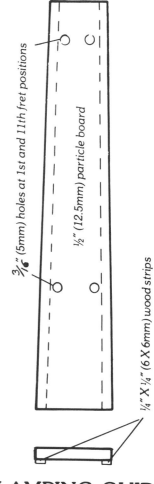

3/16" (5mm) holes at 1st and 11th fret positions

1/2" (12.5mm) particle board

1/4" X 1/4" (6 X 6mm) wood strips

CLAMPING GUIDE

Shaping
the Neck

.

Shaping the Neck:

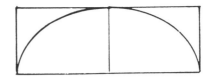

This is an area where a lot of guitar makers have difficulty and yet it is a quite straightforward procedure to both predetermine and control the shape of the neck.

A. Trim the excess wood from the neck so that it is flush with the edges of the fretboard. Make sure that the edges are at 90° to the back of the neck.

B. Mount the guitar, face down on the workboard with the neck projecting (see photo # 1). Protect the soundboard with a ¼" (6.35mm) sheet of foam rubber between it and the workboard (make sure that the foam avoids the fretboard). Clamp the area of the neck/body block with a sash cramp, using a piece of scrap wood to protect the back from being marred. Use dowel clamps to prevent the guitar from turning and hold the lower bout firm with rubber bands.

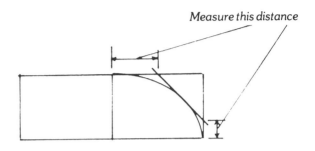

Measure this distance

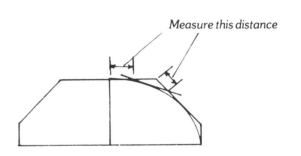

Measure this distance

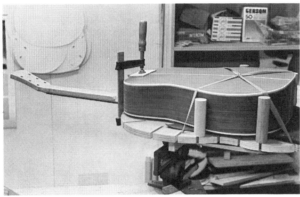

Photo # 1

C. Make sure that the centre line on the back of the neck is clearly marked.

D. Measure the width of the fretboard at the 1st and 8th frets.

E. Measure the thickness of the neck (not including the fretboard) at the 1st and 8th frets.

F. Draw a box with these dimensions for both the 1st and 8th fret positions. These represent a neck cross section (see diagram # 1).

G. Using french drawing curves, draw the shape of the neck within each box (diagram # 2 can be used as a guide).

H. Draw a tangent at 45° to the neck shape curve on both the 1st and 8th fret diagrams.

NOTE: It is only necessary to draw the tangent on one side of the curve.

I. Measure the distance from the fretboard/neck join to where the tangents intersect the side of the box diagram. Measure the distance from the centre of the back of the neck to where the tangents intersect the top of the box (see diagram # 1).

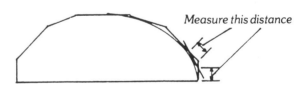

Measure this distance

Diagram # 1

J. Transfer the measurements to both sides of the neck and draw a straight line between them (see photo # 2).

Photo # 2

Photo # 3

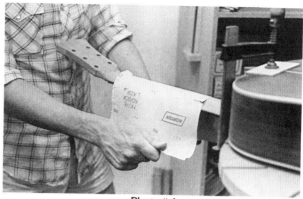

Photo # 4

K. Using a spokeshave or drawknife, plane a facet on each side of the neck down to the lines (see photo # 3). Be careful of grain tearout.

L. Draw another tangent to the neck curve on each box diagram (see diagram # 1). *(NOTE: This diagram shows the neck with one facet shaved each side).*

M. Measure the distance from the centre of the back of the neck to where this tangent intersects the top of the box. Measure the distance from where the first tangent intersects the top of the box to where the two tangents intersect (see diagram # 1).

N. Repeat steps **J** and **K** to produce the second facet.

O. Draw a third tangent to the neck curve at each position.

P. Measure the distance from the neck/fretboard join to where this tangent intersects the side of the box. Measure the distance from where the first tangent intersects the side of the box to where the first and third tangents intersect (see diagram # 1).

Q. Repeat steps **J** and **K** to produce a third facet.

R. Using the spokeshave, plane off the peaks between the facets to produce a rough curve.

S. Using a sheet of 80 grit sandpaper, sand the neck shape to a smooth curve. The motion of the sanding should be across the neck rather than along it (see photo # 4).

NOTE: Be careful not to sand too vigorously, thus removing too much wood and weakening the neck. Remove all flat spots from the facets. With the crossway motion of the sandpaper these flat spots are easy to see.

T. Using a 1″ (12.5mm) chisel followed by 120 grit sandpaper, held on the fingers, mould the neck shape gracefully into the heel shape. Its a good habit to develop the feeling of imperfections with the fingertips.

U. Mark a curve at the base of the peghead (see photo # 5). Use a chisel followed by 120 grit sandpaper to mould this to the neck curve.

V. The neck should now be sanded along the grain with 120 grit sandpaper to remove all trace of the 80 grit cross scratches.

Photo # 5

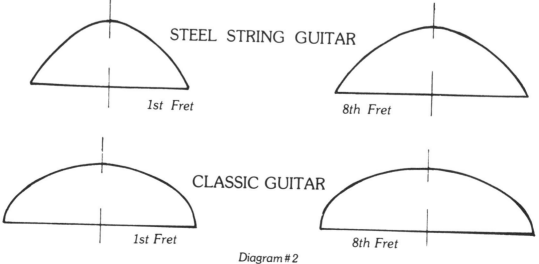

STEEL STRING GUITAR

1st Fret

8th Fret

CLASSIC GUITAR

1st Fret

8th Fret

Diagram # 2

Finishing

Finishing:

Having taken great care in constructing the guitar it is important to apply the finish in a way that will enhance its beauty. Below I have listed several different finishes and included a brief description of each.

Nitro-cellulose Lacquer; Used by makers such as C.F. Martin, Gibson and Guild, and my personal choice. Furniture grade is the most suitable for working with wood and should be sprayed on, although a brushing lacquer is a viable alternative. Nitro-cellulose can be applied thinly and, when damaged, can be easily touched up. It dries by the evaporation of thinners leaving only 30 — 35% of solids on the guitar, and is touch dry in a few minutes. Its disadvantages are its susceptibility to "blooming" (cloudiness caused by moisture trapped in the finish) when spraying in humid conditions and its high flammability. Extreme care must be taken to spray and store lacquer away from naked flame or sparks.

Polyurethane Lacquer; The most commonly used are the two pot types. These can be sprayed or brushed. Less coats are required as they dry by chemical reaction leaving around 70 — 80% solids on the guitar. Their big disadvantage is that once the chemical reaction is complete (about 24 hours) the finish can't be touched up or repaired. Polyurethane is also difficult to remove.

French Polish; A solution of shellac and methylated spirits (alcohol in the U.S.A.) which can be applied by conventional hand rubbing (a task requiring great skill) or by brushing or spraying. It is reasonably safe to work with. Its disadvantages are its susceptibility to damage from spilt liquids, its relative softness and the skill required to produce a high gloss.

Spirit and Oil Varnish; These are the more traditional finishes for musical instruments, especially of the violin family. Their disadvantage is that they are slow drying, particularly oil varnish, and as such can pick up dust particles from the air more readily. A degree of skill and patience is required to produce a high gloss but they provide a cheaper alternative because they can be brushed which eliminates the need for spraying equipment.

Acrylic Lacquer; Is favoured by many Japanese manufacturers and some solo makers. It is available in formulations to suit use on wood and is the type of lacquer used mostly to spray automobiles. It can be softened and touched up for repairs. It also dries by the evaporation of thinners and is touch dry in a few minutes. Acrylics are generally regarded as an inferior finish for guitars.

SAFETY: I cannot over emphasise the importance of developing safetyconsciousness when working with finishing products. All are flammable and in the case of spraying lacquers extremely so. Always apply lacquer in a well ventilated area and, if spraying, wear a respirator style mask suitable for noxious fumes.

Photo # 1

Spraying Equipment;

The best equipment for spraying on a small scale is also the most expensive. I use an Iwata W-71 spray gun, a Binks-Bullows water trap and pressure regulator and a hybrid 4 cubic foot/minute electric air compressor. This gives an excellent result once the technique of spraying has been mastered. (See photo # 1).

Airless spray guns, as they are called, do in fact have a tiny air piston which sprays the lacquer in short staccato bursts. They can be purchased cheaply and give quite satisfactory results. I know of a number of guitar makers who have used these to good effect although others regard them as a curse. Their big advantage is price, around a quarter of the price of a compressor outfit.

Spraying Technique;

If you peruse the employment section of any major newspaper it will become evident that spray painting is a sought after skill. The key to developing this skill is practice, just like riding a bicycle. The gun should be held around 8" (200mm) from the work and moved at such a speed as to apply the lacquer in a "wet" fashion, without dribbling. In order to determine the "wetness" of the application, good lighting is necessary to pick up the reflections on the surface as you spray. Most spray guns have an elliptical spray pattern and this should be moved as in *diagram # 1.*

Each pass of the gun should overlap the previous one by 25% and each surface should be coated twice, with each coat at 90⁰ to each other.

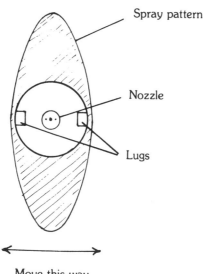

Spray pattern

Nozzle

Lugs

Move this way

Diagram # 1

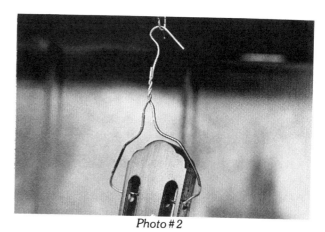

Photo # 2

Photo # 3

Holding the Guitar;

There are two good ways of doing this, the most simple being a piece of metal coathanger bent into a "V" shape and hooked through the machine head holes. (See photos # 2 & 3). The soundhole can be blocked with a balloon blown up and tied inside.

I prefer to use a clamp fixed through the soundhole with its handle mounted in a floor stand or bracket. (See diagram # 2). The soundhole can be blocked by a piece of cardboard cut around the clamp and supported by a block of foam rubber. The advantage of this method is that the largest surfaces are horizontal which reduces the risk of dribbling.

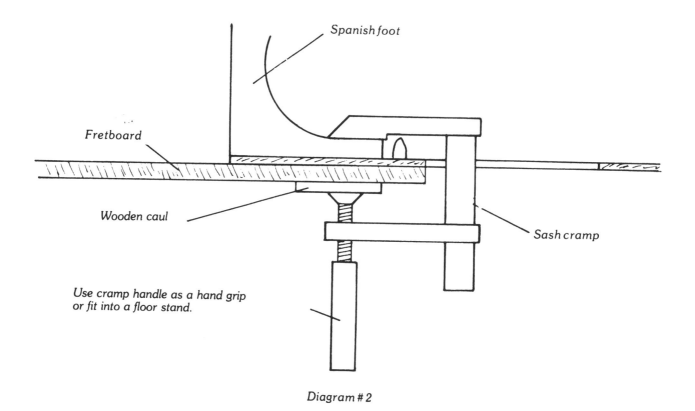

Spanish foot

Fretboard

Wooden caul

Sash cramp

Use cramp handle as a hand grip
or fit into a floor stand.

Diagram # 2

Final Sanding;

By now the use of sandpaper should be almost second nature. However, final sanding is most important as any imperfections will be highlighted, rather than hidden, by the finish.

The following procedures and precautions should be followed.

A. Always support the sandpaper with a flat block (a hard rubber sanding block is useful). The neck and heel should be hand sanded while the sanding of the waist can be effected by wrapping the paper around a dowel. Failure to support the paper will lead to undulations on the flat surfaces, particularly the soundboard.

B. Remove all traces of glue as these will show up yellow under the finish. This is most likely to occur around the bindings and purflings.

C. Don't be too zealous and sand too thin. Be mindful of the fact that the soundboard, back and sides are thin membranes.

D. Round the edges of the bindings and heel cap, and to a lesser extent the edges of the peghead. The reason for this is that lacquer doesn't adhere very satisfactorily to sharp corners and sharp corners are more easily damaged.

E. Start with 120 grit sandpaper, then proceed to 180 and finally 320 grit.

F. Take great care with the soundboard as scratches show up more readily here. After final sanding, the soundboard should be wiped over with a damp cloth to raise the grain. Allow to dry and fine sand lightly with 400 grit paper.

Procedure for Spraying Nitro-cellulose Lacquer;

NOTE: The procedure for spraying acrylic is very similar.

Set the compressor at 30-40 p.s.i. (210-280 kpa.). Spray only on dry days.

After final sanding brush or blow, with compressed air, as much dust as possible from the guitar.

A. Mask the fretboard carefully, ensuring that the masking tape leaves a thin, unmasked strip down each edge. This is to prevent chipping when the tape is removed.

B. After final sanding, brush or blow, with compressed air, as much dust as possible from the guitar.

C. Spray the whole instrument with a *light* coat of sanding sealer 30% mixed with lacquer thinners 70%.

NOTE: A thin solution of french polish also makes an excellent sealer.

D. Allow one hour to dry then apply grain filler as follows.

a. Choose an appropriate grain filler for the wood (e.g. mahogany for mahogany). A general rule is that the grain filler should be slightly darker than the timber.

b. Mask all light coloured bindings and the soundboard, as the grain filler will stain these badly. If staining does occur it can be removed with a turpentine moistened rag.

c. Work grain filler into the pores of the wood using fingertips. Work on one surface at a time.

d. Scrape off the excess grain filler, working across the grain with a small piece of posterboard.

e. Rub off the residue of thegrain filler with a piece of hessian (burlap), working across the grain.

f. Rub off the streaks from the previous step using a piece of paper towel.

g. Allow at least 24 hours for the grain filler to dry.

E. Remove the masking tape and scrape off the excess grain filler with a razor blade or hobby knife. Pay careful attention to the bindings and purflings.

F. Spray the whole guitar with another light coat of sanding sealer as in step **B.**

G. Allow one hour to dry, the apply a liberal double coat of nitro-cellulose lacquer 40% mixed with lacquer thinners 60%. Allow one hour to dry before applying the next double coat.

NOTE: No more than three double coats should be applied in one day.

H. Allow to dry overnight and apply another three double coats of the same mixture.

I. Allow to dry overnight, then sand all surfaces flat using a rubber sanding block fitted with 320 grit aluminium oxide sandpaper. (See photo # 4). Sanding flat requires the removal of all shiny spots (which indicate hollows). The neck can be sanded with the sandpaper held in the hand. The waist will require the use of a dowel.

Photo # 4

J. Apply another three double coats then allow four or five days to dry. Clean the spray gun.

K. Cut all surfaces flat using 800 grit wet or dry paper held in the rubber sanding block, as explained in step **I.** The sandpaper should be wet and lubricated with soap. A plastic bowl of water and a bar of soap is all that is needed. Wet the paper and lightly rub on the soap. Rinse the paper regularly and change frequently as it becomes clogged and ineffective.

L. Polish with a coarse cutting compound, progressing to a fine compound and then to a good quality guitar polish. Paper towel or cotton rags are best for this purpose. Use a new piece of towel or rag when changing to a finer compound.

NOTE: DO not, under any circumstances, use any cutting compound or polish containing silicones. Silicones will eventually damage the finish and make touch up or refinishing an absolute nightmare.

M. If you are feeling particularly adventurous, and can exercise great care, buffing dry with a lambswool pad held in an electric hand drill gives a mirror like lustre. (See photo # 5). Failing this, hand rubbing with tissue paper or velvet cloth produces an excellent result.

Photo # 5

Alternative Finishes;

I am indebted to Robin Moyes for this section. In addition to his guitar making skills he is a part-time lecturer in french polishing.

The aim here is to present a number of alternative finishes which avoid the use of spray equipment. Some represent a compromise in quality but all perform the function of sealing and protecting the guitar as well bringing out the natural beauty of the wood.

Shellac Finishes;

Shellac provides a versatile finshing material which can be applied by brush, rubber, swooge and/or spray gun.

NOTE: A number of different types of shellac are available which will give slightly different effects when finishing your guitar.

ORANGE SHELLAC is the most common. This produces cloudy orange polish - cloudy because it contains lac wax and will tend to yellow light coloured woods such as spruce.

DE—WAXED SHELLAC can be purchased, or made by filtering orange polish through filter paper. It is darker in colour - almost wine red - but is clear. It will polish to a higher shine than orange polish but also yellows light coloured woods.

DE—WAXED and DE—COLOURED LAC is also available from specialist suppliers. Some examples are Blonde, Super Blonde and Platina, which is the palest.

BLEACHED LAC is not recommended.

For general work 8 ozs. (250 grams) of lac should be dissolved in 32 fl.ozs. (1 litre) of methylated spirits or denatured alcohol. Stir the mixture frequently until all flakes are dissolved, then strain the mixture through fine muslin to ensure it is free of grit. Avoid metal containers which can react with and colour the polish. Glass, stainless steel or enamelled is best.

Shellac can also be used as a sealer under lacquer and oil based (traditional) grain fillers though any excessive build up of shellac should be avoided in this context. One coat is generally sufficient for sealing.

If you have used an open grain timber for the back, sides and neck then in most cases an oil based grain filler should be used. Before grain filling you should seal the guitar with a coat of shellac. This keeps the oil in the grain filler from the wood and, if used correctly, will protect light coloured bindings and purflings from pigment colour and will keep the figure of the wood clean and clear.

The *swooge* is a good way to apply sealer coats. This is simply a piece of cotton wool folded loosely to provide a clean face and fully charged with polish (I will refer to shellac dissolved in methylated spirits or denatured alcohol as "polish"). The swooge is charged by dipping into a small bowl of polish so that it is uniformly saturated and then squeezed out so that the swooge is not so wet as to be uncontrollable. On the open parts of the guitar, particularly the back, this is fine, but for awkward parts (i.e. around the heel area) the swooge needs to be considerably drier so that it can be worked with enough pressure to get into corners without excessive polish being squeezed onto the guitar.

The swooge is used along the grain and each stroke slightly overlaps the previous one. This keeps a wet edge on the coat and gives a more uniform application. The stroke is commenced an inch or two inside the end of the job and lightly stroked out to that edge; without pausing, the swooge is stroked back onto the job picking up the commencement of the previous stroke and carried through to the other end of the panel. The effect of this is to avoid pulling the swooge over the edge of guitar which can pull polish out of the swooge and cause it to run.

Coat the back and top of the guitar in the manner described, then the peghead, neck and heel with the swooge drying out or squeezed out drier if necessary. Finally coat the sides from the heel round to the butt strip in one continuous stroke.

Polish can be applied with a brush in a similar manner to the swooge, i.e. the stroke is commenced inside the edge of the job and carried out to the edge. The stroke is then picked up and carried to the other end of the job. To coat the sides next to the heel, place the brush into the corner and draw it away from the corner and with the grain.

NOTE: Special brushes are designed for applying polish. Most suitable is the blender which is a flat brush in varying widths of which 1½" - 2" (38 — 50mm) is the most suitable for a guitar. The better brushes are very soft and have sable, civett or squirrel hair while cheaper brushes use bear or goat bristles. An expensive brush is not essential, but the softer the better. These can be purchased at signwriter's supply houses, cabinet maker's suppliers and some specialty hardware stores.

After use the brush should be washed in methylated spirits or denatured alcohol, then shaped and allowed to dry undisturbed. Stand in meths, alcohol or polish to soften before re-using.

The initial sealer coat will always look somewhat streaky and no attempt should be made to even it up by brushing the polish out in the way you would with housepaint (i.e. by going back over the coat with a brush or swooge. Because the polish is very thin in body it dries very quickly. It should be simply laid on with a brush or swooge and allowed to dry. Drying time for a coat of polish is around fifteen minutes.

NOTE: Initial application of polish can also be effected with a spray gun, in which case the technique is as for spraying lacquer. Polish flows readily from the gun but doesn't set as quickly as lacquer so ensure the first coat isn't too heavy.

Using the spraygun can be an advantage on East Indian rosewood which contains a lot of soluble colour which can be dragged over the binding and purflings by the brush or swooge.

Before grain filling, it is important to ease down the first coat to remove any raised grain. Use 320 grit aluminium oxide, no-fill paper. Finally, before grain filling, any areas needing special attention can be given an extra coat, or two of polish with a pencil brush. These areas may include a rough spot of light coloured binding or purfling which could harbour pigment colour from the grain filler.

Following grain filling, the guitar is given a further coat of polish in the same way as the first coat. This provides a good base for a variety of finishes.

The quickest and easiest finish is a matt, or low gloss, finish which is achieved by brushing, or swooging, on several more coats of polish in the manner previously described. To reach the final finish, and dull the surface, rub back the finish using fine steel wool and working with the grain. Care will be needed in the heel area to avoid scratching the sides across the grain as such scratches are difficult to remove.

This cannot be regarded as a high grade finish. Nevertheless, it will adequately perform its function of protecting the guitar.

If you want to finish out to a satin finish (i.e. a finish with a gloss rating between matt and full-gloss) more work is required to close up some of the open grain still showing in the finish coats. This can be achieved by building up further coats of polish, and cutting back between coats with 320 to 400 grit aluminium oxide paper which is designed for cutting back varnish and lacquer without lubricant. Dust off the guitar thoroughly after each sanding. Open grain will show as shiny flecks where the sandpaper hasn't reached (see section on spraying nitro-cellulose).

NOTE: Although the drying time for a sealing coat of polish is only fifteen minutes, this is deceptive when further coats of polish are applied. Later coats will soften the polish already on the surface and this will slow the drying time. I suggest three coats a day as a safe maximum for average drying conditions. Poor drying conditions such as cold, damp weather or draughty conditions can cause polish to "bloom". This can be remedied by warming the work area, stopping draughts and giving the guitar a coat of polish to release the moisture.

Be wary of going back over recently coated surfaces to pick up small areas missed in the first coat. There is a real danger of dragging off polish already on the surface leaving a rough uneven coat. Should this occur, allow enough time for drying before sanding the offending area and re-coating. Polish doesn't cut back or buff as well as lacquer so using a block to back the sandpaper will cause the paper to clog. Try folding the paper and holding with the fingers and do all cutting back with the grain. As the finish builds up use a finer sandpaper to ensure that sanding scratches do not show in the final finish. I suggest using 500 and 600 grit at this stage. At least overnight drying should be allowed before final cutting back and it should not be too rigorous. Even eight to ten coats of polish will result in little build up, with cutting back between coats, and a gradual build up needs to be achieved by coating and cutting back.

Fine steel wool is again used for the final rubbing back, with a wax lubricant to protect the surface. A suitable lubricant can be made by dissolving beeswax in turpentine (mineral or vegetable) so that a soft paste results.

Dip a pad of 00 steel wool into the wax and then proceed to gently, but thoroughly, rub the finish back, always working with the grain. Finally use a soft polishing cloth to buff off the excess beeswax left on the surface. In places where the wax has solidified, and is difficult to remove, slightly moisten the cloth with turps to soften the wax. Change to a clean cloth when the old cloth becomes choked with wax.

Working With the Rubber;

The following procedure requires an experienced hand, I would suggest that you practice on flat panels before attempting the guitar. If you have any french polishing experience this procedure should present no real difficulty.

Traditional french polishing requires the use of a polishing rubber to apply the polish and the process requires the exacting application of polish in three or four separate stages. The complexities of this process are difficult to convey on paper so I have restricted myself to describing the technique of soft rubbing.·

NOTE: For further descriptions of french polishing techniques refer to the works listed below keeping in mind that some modification is required for use on guitars, the most obvious being the use of a smaller rubber.

Soft rubbing can be accomplished with either french polish alone or a mixture of polish 60% and spirit varnish 40%. Most available spirit varnishes are a relatively low grade finish and are used in conjunction with shellac. Spirit varnish improves the build of the polish and imparts a higher shine to the finish, whereas shellac improves the durability of the varnish giving it greater flexibility and reducing its tendency to scratch white.

Making the rubber;

You will need a piece of cotton wool, 4" to 5" (100 to 125mm) square and a piece of close weave cotton (e.g. pillow case) 10" to 12" (250 to 300mm) square.

First, take the cotton wool and gently roll the edges under while rotating the piece in your hands. This will form the cotton wool into a pad with a smooth face (see step # 1). Pick a section of the pad that will form easily to a point, or toe, and mould the cotton wool around this into a half pear shape. Place the cloth over the face of the pad, and hold the cloth and pad between forefinger and thumb with the toe of the rubber pointing in the same direction as the thumb and forefinger (see step # 2). Pinch the top of the rubber into shape so that the cloth, at the toe, can be folded back along the body of the rubber (see step # 3). Transfer the rubber to the other hand, holding the rubber with the fold under the thumb, and take two more folds back over the first fold, running in the same direction (see step # 4). Gather the loose cloth on top of the rubber (part of which includes the cloth you have folded back away from the toe of the rubber) and wrap it around itself so that the rubber shape is formed. The cloth can be tucked under its own folds so that it stays tied, then mould the rubber to a slightly better shape; a broad half pear shape with a flat working surface which is *free of folds* and has a well formed point or toe. Folds on the rubber face will scratch the polish surface, and the toe is necessary for access to corners of the guitar.

This rubber is used well charged and should not be tied too tightly. Try tying it dry first until you are getting reasonable results before untying the rubber and charging the core with polish, through the back. Saturate the cotton wool and re-tie the rubber (it moulds to shape easier when wet but gets messy). Squeeze the rubber out slightly on a piece of newspaper before applying it to your guitar so that unmanageable amounts of polish don't come out of the rubber when you start polishing.

Start polishing on the back of the guitar first — its open and has no awkward corners. Move the rubber in steady, open, circular movements, keeping it moving at all times. Make sure you glide it onto and off the guitar. Make sure the polish isn't coming out in swirls, but in smooth, even, light coats. You need good light to see what is happening on the surface of the guitar. If the rubber is leaving swirls of polish then it is too wet for the amount of pressure you are using. Either squeeze the rubber out a little, or ease up on the pressure until the rubber dries out somewhat. Be wary of the surface getting soft and sticky; when it does move on to another part of the guitar and allow time for the first section to dry. Rubber marks can be straightened out throughout the process but avoid excessive working with the grain as this will cause a "ropey" appearance on the finish.

As the rubber dries out, use the toe to start working into the corners formed where the fretboard covers the soundboard and next to the heel. Don't leave these spots too late in the process as they should blend into the general finish.

Using the rubber tends to push the polish into the grain, but best results will be achieved by carrying out polishing over a number of days and cutting back lightly before polishing each day. Use worn 240 or 320 grit paper for this, rubbing two pieces face to face to reduce the cut. Do all cutting with the grain and dust off before commencing polishing. In cutting back, pay attention to any rough patches caused by allowing the polish to get too soft during polishing. Spots that appear dull compared to to the rest of the surface probably indicate areas where you have pulled the polish back off the surface with the rubber. Be aware of the polish surface as you work and go on to other areas of the guitar before the area you are working on becomes too soft.

As your skill develops you will be able to achieve a good final finish off the rubber. If you have a good build up of polish on the guitar but find it difficult to get a good finish off the rubber then you can use the steel wool and wax technique already described. Following that you can use burnishing fluid (sold by cabinet maker's suppliers) to give a final polish.

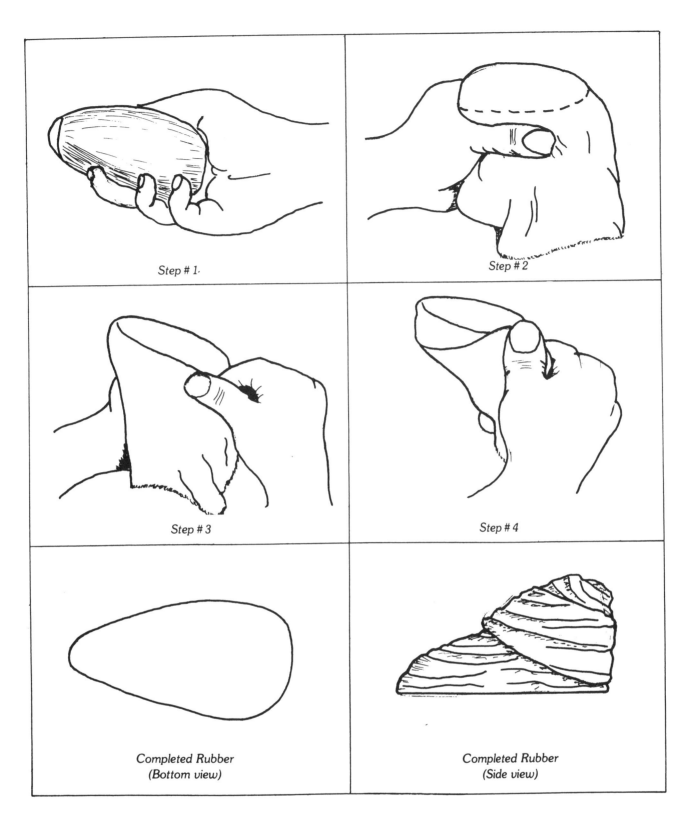

Step # 1.

Step # 2

Step # 3

Step # 4

Completed Rubber
(Bottom view)

Completed Rubber
(Side view)

NOTE: Burnishing fluid is designed for use on shellac finishes and is a fine cutting compound using Keiselguhr or Tripoli powder as its cutting agent. Be sure not use finishing spirits which is designed for use on lacquer. It contains meths which will soften the finish. The wax and steel wool technique will help cover blemishes providing you are getting even coverage with the rubber. Burnisher will not cover rubber marks but it will polish out the scratches and give a good degree of gloss. Apply burnisher to a soft cloth (e.g. flanelette) and work it vigorously in circles, and then with the grain, before wiping off.

As I have said, the technique of soft rubbing can be used for a spirit varnish/polish mixture as well as for straight polish. The varnish mixture feels stickier under the rubber and therefore is less comfortable to work with. It tends to give a more rapid build, and higher gloss, than soft rubbing with polish alone. However, the techniques are the same for either mixture.

Brushing Lacquer;

Some paint companies manufacture nitro-cellulose lacquers which have slow solvents and can be brushed, rather than sprayed. This represents a finish which can also be applied over a base of shellac sealer and grain filler.

In applying this lacquer, use a good quality paint brush and brush the lacquer out carefully to achieve an even coat. Try not to work the lacquer for too long as there is a danger of tearing the finish, or pulling hairs from the brush as it begins to firm.

Brushing lacquer can be cut back in the same way as spraying lacquers, using wet or dry paper and appropriate lubricants. However, it is a softer lacquer than spraying lacquer and cannot be buffed as vigorously. Don't expect to achieve as high a gloss and be careful not to burn and soften the finish when compounding. The number of coats needed is dependent on a number of factors; how full a finish you desire and how open the grain of the timber. For soundboards, three or four coats should be enough to achieve a full finish, whereas open grain hardwoods may require six to eight coats. I suggest cutting back thoroughly between coats, using 320 grit aluminium oxide paper backed with a rubber sanding block. This will make final cutting back easier and make it more obvious when sufficient coats have been applied.

The characteristic softness of brushing lacquer means that it works well with a pulling rubber and can be pulled in with a rubber tied in genuine chamois and charged with a mixture of 50% methylated spirits, or denatured alcohol and 50% lacquer thinners. Alternatively the rubber can be tied with linen and charged with a mixture of lacquer and thinners. In both cases the rubber is tied in the fashion as a soft rubber for polishing, though it needs to be tied more firmly and used a lot drier. The benefit of the rubber is that with two or three coats of lacquer brushed onto the guitar, the rubber can be used to work the lacquer and this chokes up the grain as the lacquer is pushed into the pores.

NOTE: As for rubber work with polish, the lacquer rubber, or pulling rubber, is worked principally in circles. Excessive working with the grain will pull lacquer out of the grain. The pulling rubber needs to be worked with more weight, but remain aware of the fragile nature of the guitar.

It is possible to achieve a good finish "off the rubber" although some shrinkback can be expected as the solvents evaporate. However, if this becomes excessive, the finish can be cut back and re-worked with the rubber, or carefully compounded as for spraying lacquer. Brushing lacquer requires a longer drying time between coats, and before cutting and buffing.

Other Finishes;

There are many finishes available which will do the job of sealing and protecting your guitar. Lacquer, and shellac based finishes are traditionally accepted and don't break important rules for finishing guitars (i.e. you should not use finishing materials which cannot be stripped off or repaired). However, many other finishes are satisfactory if used with care and some finesse. *Instant Estapol* which is described by the manufacturer Wattyl as "an oil modified urethane" varnish can be used to produce a full finish with good lustre if rubbed back carefully between coats and then finished with steel wool and wax, as described earlier for shellac. It can be stripped off if damaged and re-coated for repairs. It is compatible with shellac as a sealer providing the sealer coats are kept thin, and providing the finish is not exposed to to extremes of heat and sunlight. This is given as an example of a finish which is readily available from any hardware store, and while the purists may shudder at the thought of "estapolling a guitar" my contention is that it is capable of doing the job.

A list of publications which go into greater detail than is possible here is listed below for those who wish to further explore the world of lacquers and varnishes. Most paint manufacturers have a technical department to provide information about their products. For obvious reasons, the technical staff will err on the side of caution; for instance many paint companies don't recommend the use of shellac as a sealer under their lacquers and yet this is something which is widely taught and practiced in the field.

May your finishes never crack, craze or blister!

Further Reading;

WOOD FINISHING, by Collier, published by Perganon Press.

COLORING, FINISHING AND PAINTING WOOD, by Newell and Holtrop, published by Bennett.

THE DEPT. OF LABOUR & INDUSTRY BOOK OF FRENCH POLISHING, available from the Polishing Section, Dept. of Building, Sydney Technical College, Sydney, N.S.W., Australia.

The Bridge

The Bridge:

The bridges of nylon string and steel string guitars are quite different in construction and each has a separate method.

Steel String Guitar:

A. Cut out a posterboard template using the bridge diagram as a guide.

B. To determine the thickness of the bridge, lay a straight edge along the centre of the fretboard and measure the distance between the bottom of the straight edge and the soundboard at the approximate location of the bridge (see photo # 1).

Photo # 1

C. Take a suitable rosewood or ebony bridge blank, sand one large surface flat and sand one edge straight and at 90⁰ to the flat surface.

D. Plane the blank to its approximate thickness.

E. Mark out the shape of the bridge and the position of the bridge pin holes on the rough planed surface of the blank (a yellow or white pencil is most useful). (See photo # 2).

F. Drill the bridge pin holes with a $\frac{3}{16}$ (5mm) drill bit. *(NOTE: The accuracy of these holes is vital to even string spacing).*

Photo # 2

G. Cut the bridge to shape and sand the edges smooth.

H. Chisel and sand the "wings" of the bridge then contour the main section (see front elevation diagram # 1).

I. Taper the end profile (see end elevation, diagram # 1).

J. Cut the saddle slot $\frac{3}{16}$ (5mm) deep and $\frac{3}{16}$ X $2\frac{3}{4}$" (5 X 70mm). (See diagram # 1). This can be done with a sharp knife and chisel using the edge of a cabinet scraper as a guide or, with a dremel moto-tool and router base (see photo # 3).

Photo # 3

K. Sand all surfaces smooth using 120 grit sandpaper and progressing through 180 up to 320 grit.

Nylon String Guitar:

A. Determine the thickness of the bridge using the same basic procedure as for steel string guitar. Add $\frac{1}{8}$" (3mm) to the measurement to obtain the thickness of the bridge.

B. Plane the rosewood bridge blank to thickness and sand both surfaces flat.

C. Using the dimensions on the diagram, saw and plane the blank to width. Mark and cut to length making sure that the ends are square to the edges.

D. Mark the length of the tie-block and, using a fine backsaw, cut the profile of the wings.

E. Shape the profile of the wings using a chisel followed by 120 grit sandpaper on the small sanding block. Bevel the ends in the same way (see diagram # 1 and photo # 4).

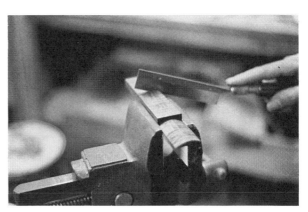

Photo # 4

F. Mark the position of the string holes and drill with a ¹⁄₁₆″ (2mm) bit. The accurate positioning of these holes is critical to string spacing. These holes should be ½″ deep.
holes should be ½″ (12.5mm) deep.

G. Using a fine backsaw and a ½″ (12.5mm) chisel, shape the valley until the string holes are revealed.

H. Mark and cut the saddle slot using a fine backsaw and 2mm chisel.

I. The edges of the tie-block are bound with bone to prevent wear and the rebates for this should also be cut with a fine backsaw and narrow chisel.

J. Make the two pieces of bone for the tie-block from a bridge saddle blank, making sure the two edges are straight and at 90⁰ to each other.

K. Glue the two pieces of bone in position with 5 minute epoxy or cyanoacrylate (super glue).

L. Sand the whole bridge smooth working up to 320 grit sandpaper.

M. The bridge, with the exception of the glueing surface, should be finished using the same procedure as for the body of the guitar. A piece of 1″ (25mm) dowel, stuck to the bottom of the bridge with double sided tape, makes a useful handle when spraying.

Fitting the Bridge

To find the correct location of the bridge the front of the saddle slot should be used for all measurement.

Steel String Guitar:

The distance from the nut end of the fretboard to the front edge of the saddle slot should be double the distance from the nut to the centre of the 12th fret PLUS ¹⁄₁₆″ (1.5mm). In plain terms this is the scale length of the guitar, plus ¹⁄₁₆″ (1.5mm) string compensation.

A. Using a suitable rule, locate the bridge in its correct position.

B. Use a small, clear plastic, protractor or set square to check that the bridge is perpendicular to the centre line of the soundboard. Tape the set square in position (see photo # 5).

Photo # 5

C. Check that the bridge is centred correctly in relation to the fretboard. This is accomplished by laying a straight edge along each edge of the fretboard in turn, and ensuring that the distance between the straight edge and the outer bridge pin holes is the same on both the bass and treble sides.

D. Clamp the bridge in position with a deep throat clamp and check its alignment again. Drill a ³⁄₁₆″ (5mm) hole through each of the outer bridge pin holes so that it passes right through the soundboard and bridge plate.

E. Remove the clamp and set square and bolt the bridge in position using ³⁄₁₆″ (5mm) gutter bolts and nuts.

F. Scribe around the edge of the bridge with a sharp knife. Take great care and use only sufficient pressure to cut through the lacquer. (See photo # 6).

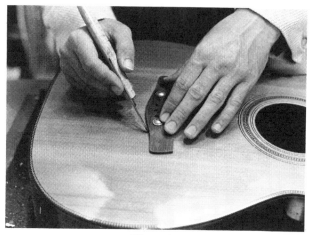

Photo # 6

G. Remove the bridge and use a ½″ (12.5mm) chisel to remove the lacquer neatly from the bridge area. Take great care not to remove too much wood from the soundboard. photo # 7).

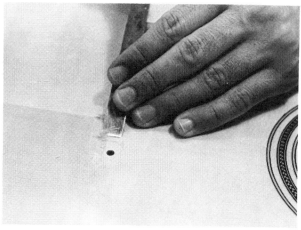

Photo # 7

H. Leach the base of the bridge with acetone and apply Titebond in sufficient quantity to cover the surface but not enough to cascade over the soundboard when clamped.

I. Clamp the bridge in position using the two gutter bolts, plus a deep throat clamp on each of the wings (see photo # 8). Clean up the excess glue carefully so as to avoid marring the finish.

Photo # 8

J. When dry, remove all the clamps and bolts and drill the remaining bridge pin holes.

K. Wash off the excess glue with a paper towel moistened with warm water.

L. Fit the bridge pins using a tapered reamer (see photo # 9).

Photo # 9

M. Slightly countersink the bridge pin holes and cut a string slot using a ground down jig saw blade (see photo # 10). Cut the string ramps using a sharp, narrow knife blade.

NOTE: Allow at least 12 hours between glueing the bridge and fitting the strings.

Photo # 10

Nylon String Guitar

A. Drill a small hole through the bottom of the saddle slot, at each end, big enough to fit a small nail (a brad) and tap a nail into each hole with its point just protruding from the bottom of the bridge.

B. Locate the bridge following steps **A** and **B** for steel string guitar.

C. Check the alignment of the bridge as in step **C** for steel string guitar utilising the string holes in the tie-block as a guide.

D. Clamp the bridge in position making sure that the point of the nails enter the soundboard.

E. Scribe around the bridge carefully, using a sharp knife to cut the lacquer only. The clamp will have to be removed to scribe the front edge so hold the bridge with your free hand.

F. Remove the lacquer from the bridge area with a sharp ½" (12.5mm) chisel.

G. Leach the base of the bridge with acetone and apply a sufficient amount of Titebond.

H. Clamp in position using three deep throat clamps. Take particular care not to damage the internal braces and ensure that the "wings" are glued (see photo # 11).

I. Allow at least one hour to dry, remove the clamps and clean up the excess glue with a cloth moistened with warm water.

J. Carefully remove the locating nails.

NOTE: Allow at least 12 hours between glueing the bridge and fitting the strings.

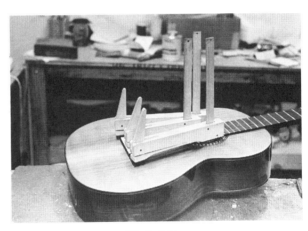

Photo # 11

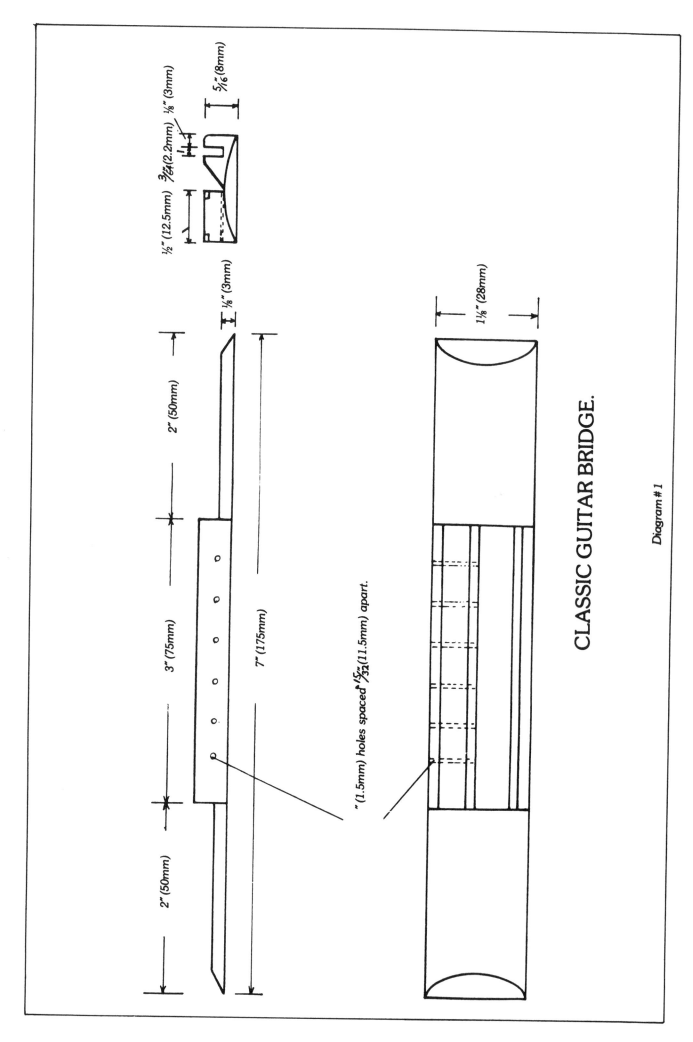

5/16" (8mm)

1/8" (3mm)

3/64" (2.2mm)

1/2" (12.5mm)

1/8" (3mm)

2" (50mm)

3" (75mm)

7" (175mm)

2" (50mm)

1 1/8" (28mm)

" (1.5mm) holes spaced 15/32" (11.5mm) apart.

CLASSIC GUITAR BRIDGE.

Diagram # 1

78

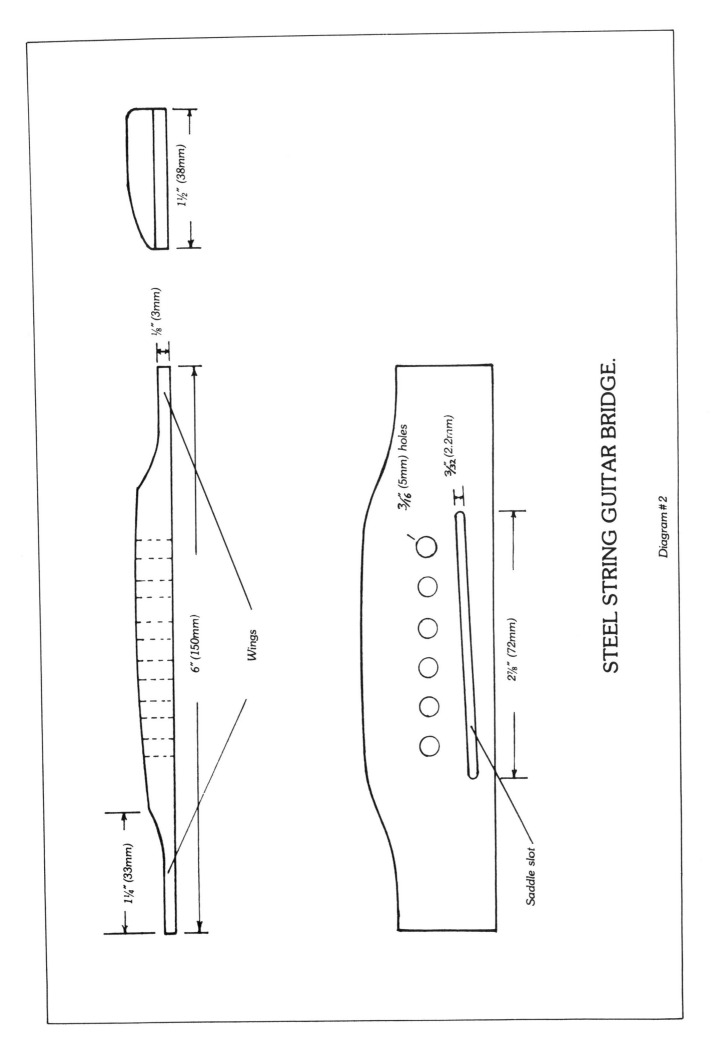

1½" (38mm)

⅛" (3mm)

6" (150mm)

Wings

1¼" (33mm)

3⁄16" (5mm) holes

3⁄32" (2.2mm)

2⅞" (72mm)

Saddle slot

STEEL STRING GUITAR BRIDGE.

Diagram # 2

Notes:

Setting Up
the Guitar
for Playing

Setting Up the Guitar for Playing:

Levelling the Frets:

A. Remove the masking tape from the fretboard.

B. Make a posterboard mask to protect the finish around the fretboard (see photo # 1).

C. Take a flat, smooth 12″ (300mm) mill file and level the top of the frets until all frets are of even height. The file marks are readily visible and will serve as a guide. Each fret should have at least a light file mark right across it.

Photo # 1

D. Smooth out the file marks using a fine india honing stone.

E. Recurve the crown, or peak, of the frets using a special fret file (see diagram # 1). Take special care to round off the sharp ends of the frets.

F. Hold a piece of folded 400grit sandpaper in your fingers and rub lengthways along the fretboard so that it polishes the frets. Repeat the process with 800 and 1200 grit.

G. Clean and oil the fretboard, in one process, with lemon oil or raw linseed oil applied with a paper towel.

Fitting the Nut:

A. . Clean the excess glue, filler etc. from the nut slot, taking care not to chip the surrounding finish.

B. File a suitable bone nut blank to fit the nut slot, mark and cut to length and file the ends smooth.

C. Mark the approximate height of the nut at   ″ (2mm) above the end of the fretboard. File the nut to this height, tapering to conform to the angle of the peghead (see diagram # 1).

D. Mark the position of the string slots and start each slot with a shallow cut using a fine backsaw.

E. Cut each slot to depth using a suitable file for the thickness of each string. Check the correct depth with a thin rule placed between the string slot and the 2nd fret. In this position, the rule should just clear the 1st fret (see diagram # 1).

*NOTE: After step **C.** the nut may need to be held in place with a drop of cyanoacrylate (super glue).*

The machine heads should be fitted at this point.

The Bridge Saddle:

The height of the bridge saddle is the chief factor in determining the action of the guitar.

Fit a posterboard protector around the bridge while working.

Steel String Guitar:

A. Make two wooden shims ½″ X 1″ (12.5 X 25mm). One should be $\frac{3}{64}$ (1.2mm) thick and the other $\frac{5}{64}$ (2mm) thick.

B. Place the thinner shim on top of the 12th fret on the treble side.

C. Lay a straight edge from the bridge to the 1st fret with one end resting on the 1st fret and the middle resting on the shim on the 12th fret. This should be in the approximate treble E string position.

D. Measure the distance from the bottom of the straight edge to the bottom of the saddle slot (see photo # 2). This will be the height of the bridge saddle at the treble side.

Photo # 2

E. Repeat this procedure for the bass side using the thicker shim.

F. Cut and sand the bone bridge blank to fit the saddle slot.

G. Mark the height of the saddle at the treble and bass ends and, using an old curved bridge saddle as a guide, mark the curve of the top of the saddle (see photo # 3).

Photo # 3

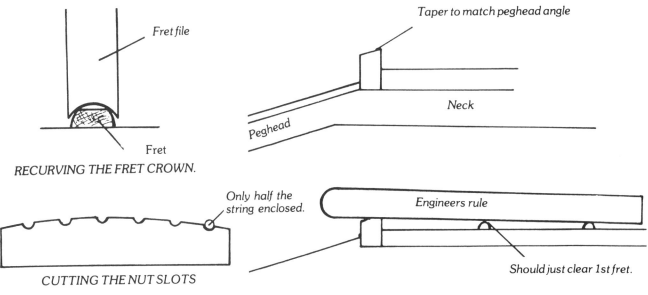

Fret file

Fret

RECURVING THE FRET CROWN.

Taper to match peghead angle

Neck

Peghead

Only half the string enclosed.

CUTTING THE NUT SLOTS

Engineers rule

Should just clear 1st fret.

Diagram # 1

H. File the height of the bridge saddle to the curve and fit the saddle to the bridge. Remove the protector.

COMPENSATING THE BRIDGE SADDLE:

NOTE: Light guage strings (12 to 52) are the most suitable for the soundboard dimensions used.

I. Fit all strings loosely and, using offcuts from the B string, make six wire hooks to fit under the strings (see diagram # 2).

J. Fit a hook under each string where it crosses the bridge saddle (see diagram # 2).

K. Use an electronic tuner to tune all strings to concert pitch.

L. Play the open treble E string and adjust it to pitch, then play the same string fretted at the 12th fret. If the fretted note is sharp the wire hook will need to be moved toward the bridge pins. If flat, toward the soundhole. Repeat the process until the fretted note and the open note are exactly one octave apart.

M. Repeat this process for all strings and mark the positions of the wire hooks with a pencil. Also mark the mid position between the strings.

N. Remove the strings and place the bridge saddle in a vise. File peaks at each string position to correspond with the position of the wire hooks (see photo # 4).

Photo # 4

O. Restring and tune to concert pitch. Check the action at the 12th fret. The clearance between the top of the fret and the bottom of the string should be $5/64''$ (2mm) on the treble E and $7/64''$ (2.8mm) on the bass E. If it needs to be lowered, remove the bridge saddle and file away its bottom surface. Replace, retune and recheck.)3P. Check the neck by placing a 12" (300mm)

P. Check the neck by placing a 12" (300mm) rule between the 1st and 12th frets and measuring the clearance above the 5th fret. This should be close to 0.016" (0.4mm). Should the neck curve be greater than this, release the string tension and tighten the truss rod one quarter of a turn. Retune the guitar and recheck.

Q. The instrument is now complete save for fitting a pickguard if required.

NOTE: The action at the 12th fret is given at $5/64''$ (2mm) on the treble E string and $7/64''$ (2.8mm) on the bass E string. Obviously, this can be varied to suit individual playing styles. The reason that the two wooden shims are made $3/64''$ (1.2mm) and $5/64''$ (2mm) thick, respectively, is to take into the slight bowing of the neck which occurs under the tension of steel strings.

Classic Guitar:

A. Make two wooden shims $1/2''$ X 1" (12.5 X 25mm); one $1/8''$ (3.2mm) thick and the other $5/32''$ (4mm) thick.

B. Place the thinner shim on the 12th fret on the treble side.

C. Lay a straight edge on the treble side in the approximate position of the E string. The straight edge should contact the 1st fret and the shim and pass over the bridge.

D. Measure the distance from the bottom of the straight edge to the bottom of the saddle slot (see photo # 2). This will be the thickness of the saddle at the treble end.

E. Repeat this procedure for the bass side.

F. Cut and sand the bridge blank to fit the saddle slot.

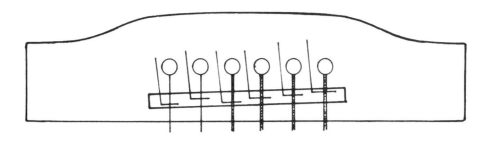

Diagram # 2

G. Mark the height of the treble and bass ends, draw a straight line between these points and sand the height of the bridge saddle to this line.
H. Round the top of the saddle to minimise string wear.
I. Fit the strings, tune to concert pitch and check the action at the 12th fret. This should be ⅛" (3.2mm) on the treble E string and $^5\!/_{32}$" (4mm) on the bass E string. If the action is too high, release the string tension, remove the saddle and sand its bottom surface. Retune and recheck.

The guitar is now complete.

Notes:

Fitting a
Florentine
Cutaway

Fitting a Florentine Cutaway:

I don't recommend that anyone attempt a cutaway on their first instrument. The additional woodwork involved is quite tricky and best left until your skills are well established.

When bending the sides for a cutaway guitar, ensure that the maximum overhang exists where the sides meet the neck rather than at the butt. The purpose of this is to provide a sufficient length of timber to make a cutaway.

A. Mark the outline of the cutaway on the template.

B. Place the side to be cutaway on the template and mark the point of intersection of the cutaway and the side. Draw a line perpendicular to this point. (See photo # 1).

C. Cut the side to this line being careful not to chip or split it.

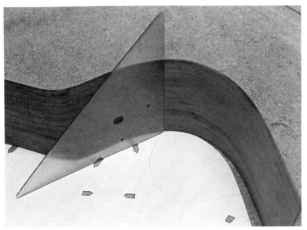

Photo # 1

D. Cut the binding about ½" (12.5mm) longer.

E. Using the plumbers butane torch and hot copper pipe, bend the off-cut side to conform to the shape of the cutaway. Be sure to use pieces of scrap timber to distribute the hand pressure when bending as short lengths like this split very easily.

F. Bend the bindings to match.

G. Using the centre line as a guide, mark the outline of the fretboard on the upper bout veneer on the inside of the soundboard.

H. Using the outline of the fretboard as a guide, mark the outline of the cutaway on the soundboard and cut to shape (see photo # 2).

I. Clamp the soundboard in position on the workboard and clamp the neck in position. (Use posterboard protectors).

Photo # 2

J. Mark the places where the cutaway curve intersects the spanish foot (see photo # 3).

Photo # 3

K. Remove the neck and mark the curve of the required cutout, using the cutaway section of the side as a template. Keep in mind that the *OUTER* surface of the side should sit flush with the fretboard at the neck/body join.

L. Chisel the correct curve into the spanish foot (see photo # 4). Make sure to retain a perpendicular relationship to the neck surface (see photo # 5).

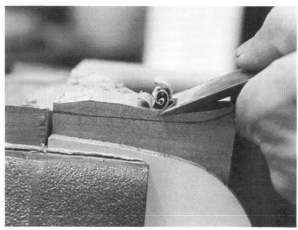

Photo # 4

Photo # 5

M. Proceed with step **I** from the **Assembly** chapter.

N. Take a piece of mahogany 4″ X ¾″ X ¾″ (100 X 19 X 19mm) and square one end to its sides. This will be the reinforcing block for the point of the cutaway.

O. Shape the block to accomodate both the main part of the side and the cutaway (see diagram # 1).

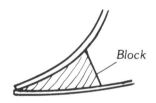

Block

Diagram # 1

P. Glue the block in place, making sure that it stands perpendicular to the soundboard.

Q. Glue the cutaway section of the side in position (see photo # 6).

Photo # 6

R. Return to the **Assembly** procedure from step **J.** The only difference being that a short section of the side will be required in the side slot at the neck/body join on the cutaway side.

S. Refer to step **AF** from the **Assembly** chapter; mark the cutaway on the back and cut out on a band saw or with a coping saw.

T. When fitting the bindings, the channels will have to be cut by hand near the ends of the cutaway as the router cannot be manouvered into these extremities safely.

U. Extra binding will have to be fitted to both the point of the cutaway and near the neck/body join.

V. The surface of the reinforcing block, at the point of the cutaway, should be prepared before glueing on the back. It should be around ⁵⁄₁₆″ (8mm) wide and perpendicular to the soundboard.

W. Cut the binding for the point of the cutaway from a piece of timber which matches the existing binding. It should be around ⅜″ X ⅜″ (10 X 10mm) and shaped to fit (see diagram # 2).

X. Glue the bindings at both ends of the cutaway only after the main binding is complete.

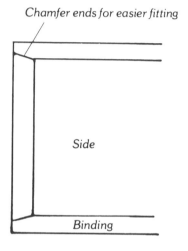

Chamfer ends for easier fitting

Side

Binding

Diagram # 2

Jigs

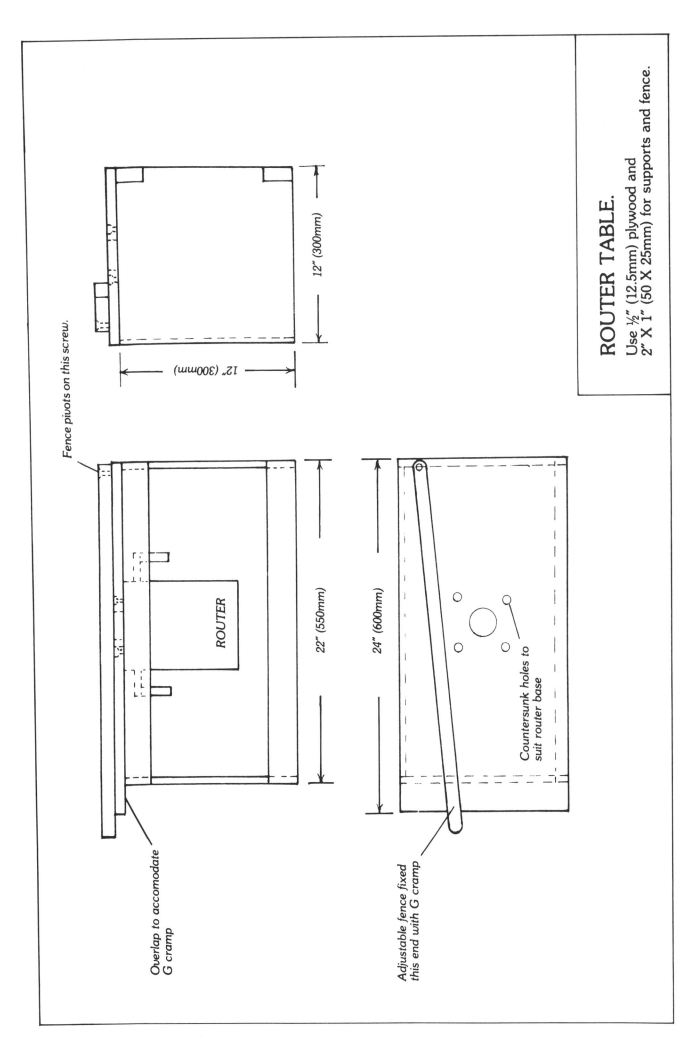

ROUTER TABLE.

Use ½" (12.5mm) plywood and
2" X 1" (50 X 25mm) for supports and fence.

Fence pivots on this screw.

12" (300mm)

12" (300mm)

ROUTER

22" (550mm)

24" (600mm)

Countersunk holes to
suit router base

Overlap to accomodate
G cramp

Adjustable fence fixed
this end with G cramp

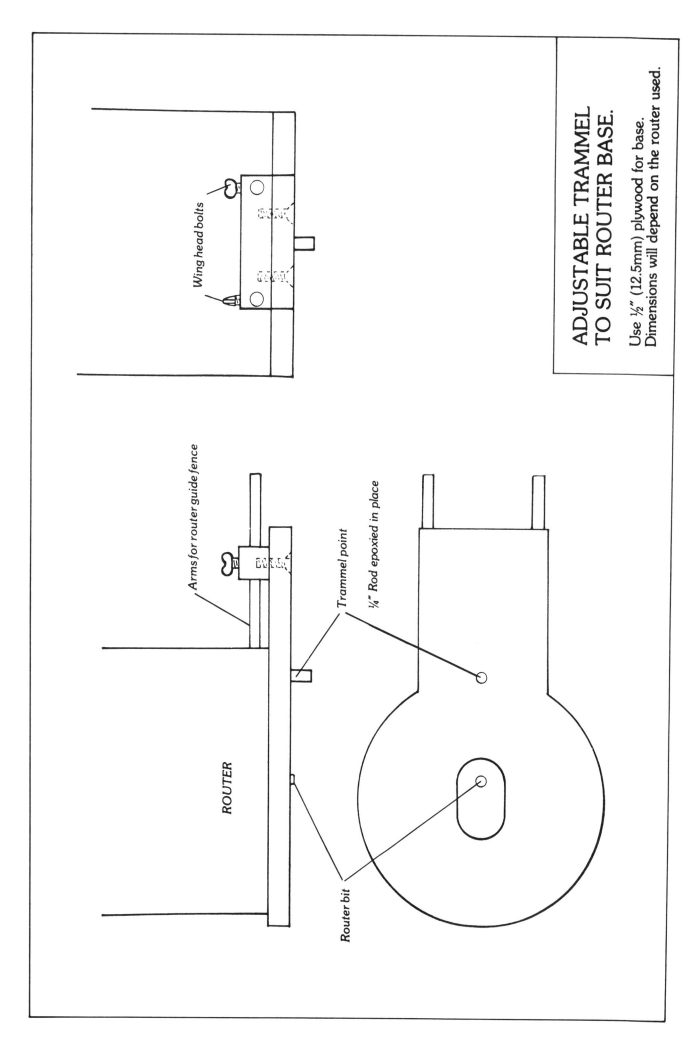

ADJUSTABLE TRAMMEL
TO SUIT ROUTER BASE.

Use ½" (12.5mm) plywood for base.
Dimensions will depend on the router used.

Wing head bolts

Arms for router guide fence

Trammel point

¼" Rod epoxied in place

ROUTER

Router bit

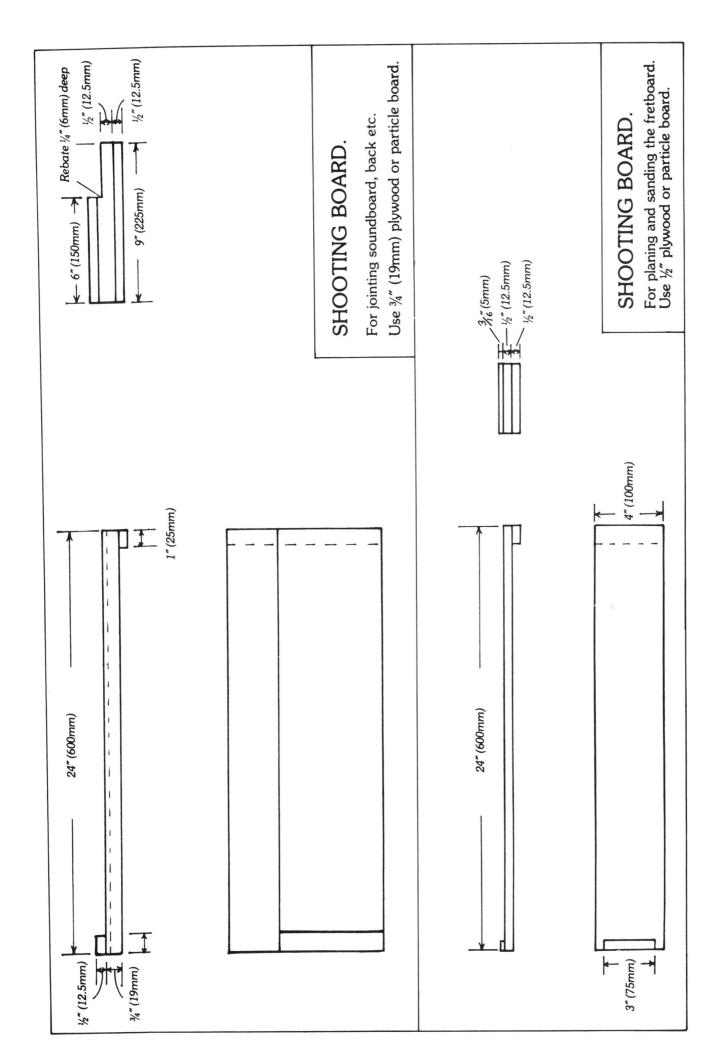

SHOOTING BOARD.

For jointing soundboard, back etc.

Use 3/4" (19mm) plywood or particle board.

SHOOTING BOARD.

For planing and sanding the fretboard.

Use 1/2" plywood or particle board.

Rebate 1/4" (6mm) deep

1/2" (12.5mm)

1/2" (12.5mm)

6" (150mm)

9" (225mm)

1" (25mm)

24" (600mm)

1/2" (12.5mm)

3/4" (19mm)

3/16" (5mm)

1/2" (12.5mm)

1/2" (12.5mm)

4" (100mm)

24" (600mm)

3" (75mm)

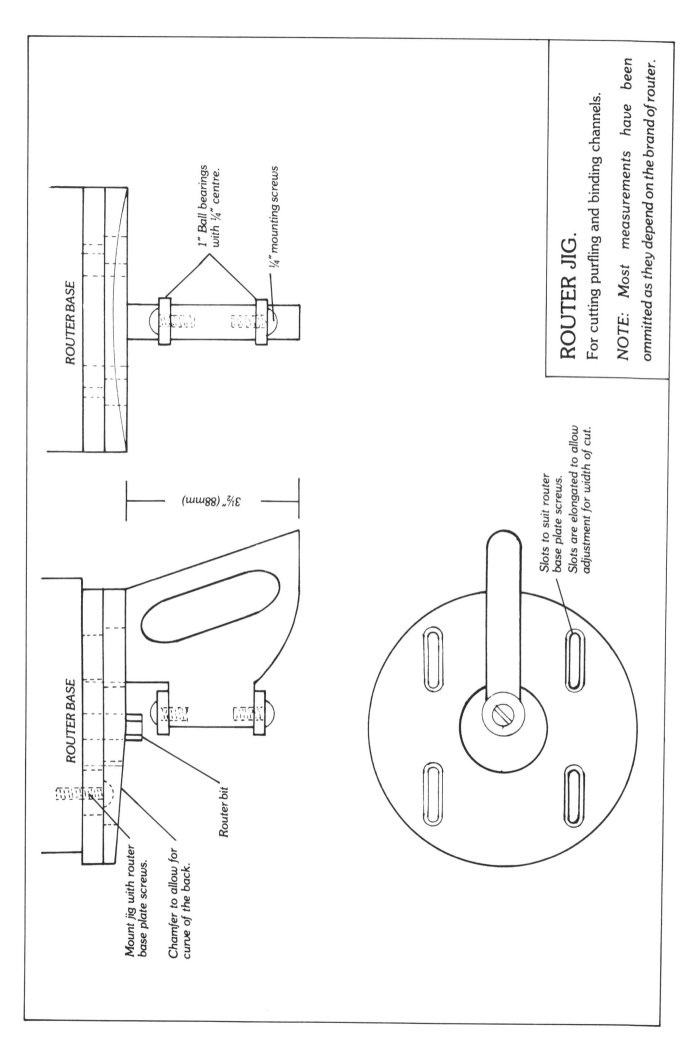

ROUTER BASE

1" Ball bearings with ¼" centre.

¼" mounting screws

3½" (88mm)

ROUTER BASE

Mount jig with router base plate screws.

Chamfer to allow for curve of the back.

Router bit

Slots to suit router base plate screws. Slots are elongated to allow adjustment for width of cut.

ROUTER JIG.

For cutting purfling and binding channels.

NOTE: Most measurements have been ommitted as they depend on the brand of router.

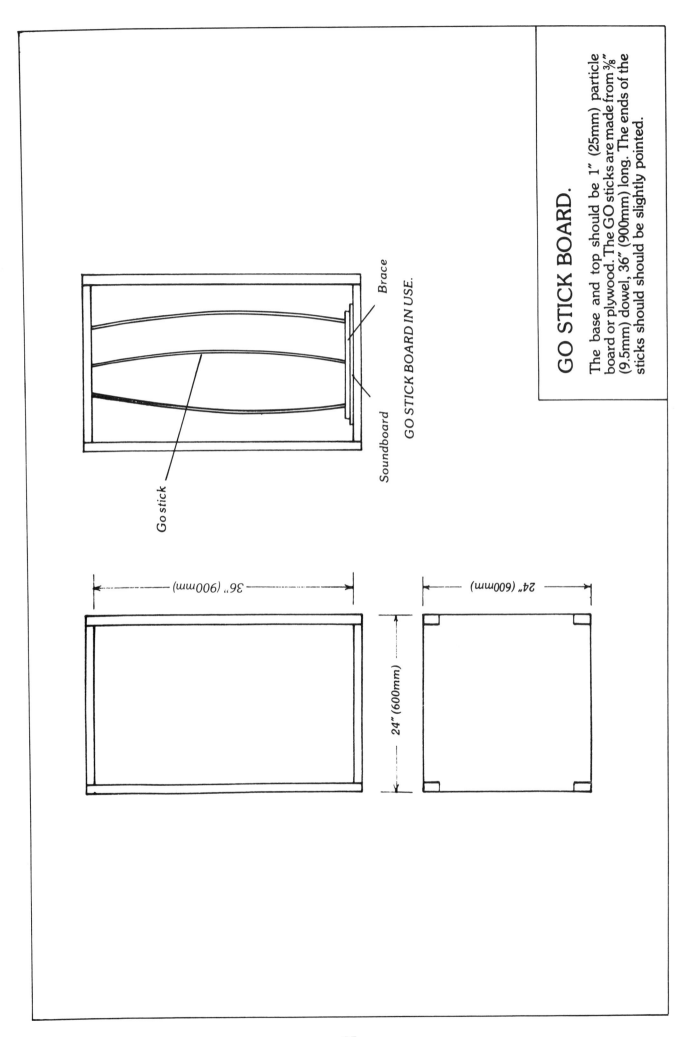

GO STICK BOARD.

The base and top should be 1" (25mm) particle board or plywood. The GO sticks are made from 3/8" (9.5mm) dowel, 36" (900mm) long. The ends of the sticks should should be slightly pointed.

Brace

GO STICK BOARD IN USE.

Soundboard

Go stick

36" (900mm)

24" (600mm)

24" (600mm)

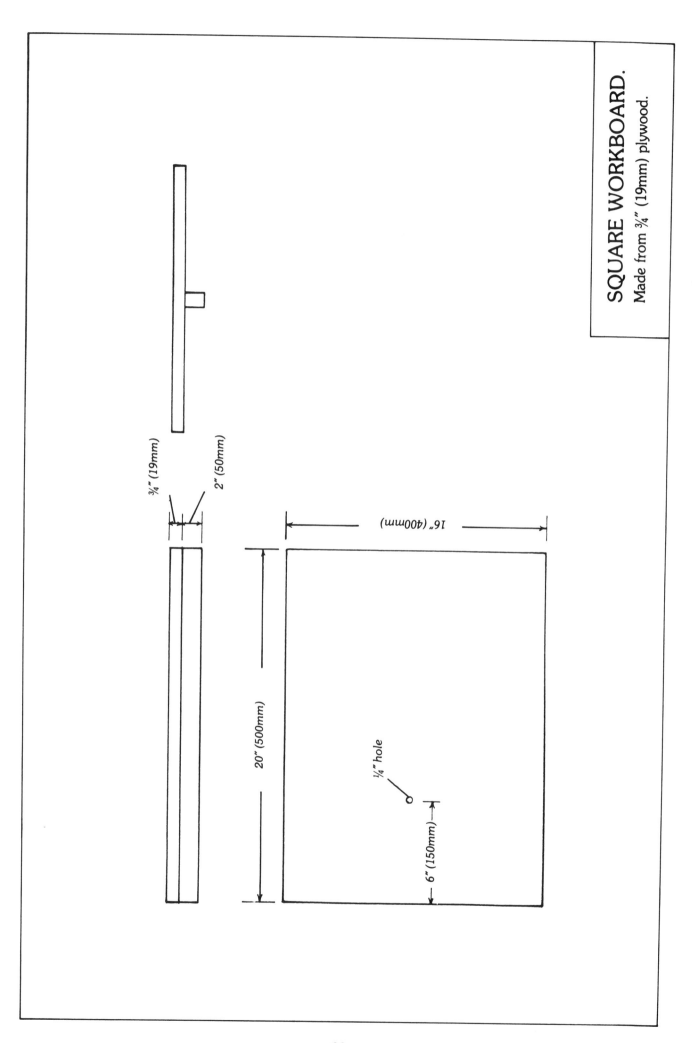

SQUARE WORKBOARD.
Made from ¾" (19mm) plywood.

¾" (19mm)

2" (50mm)

16" (400mm)

20" (500mm)

¼" hole

6" (150mm)

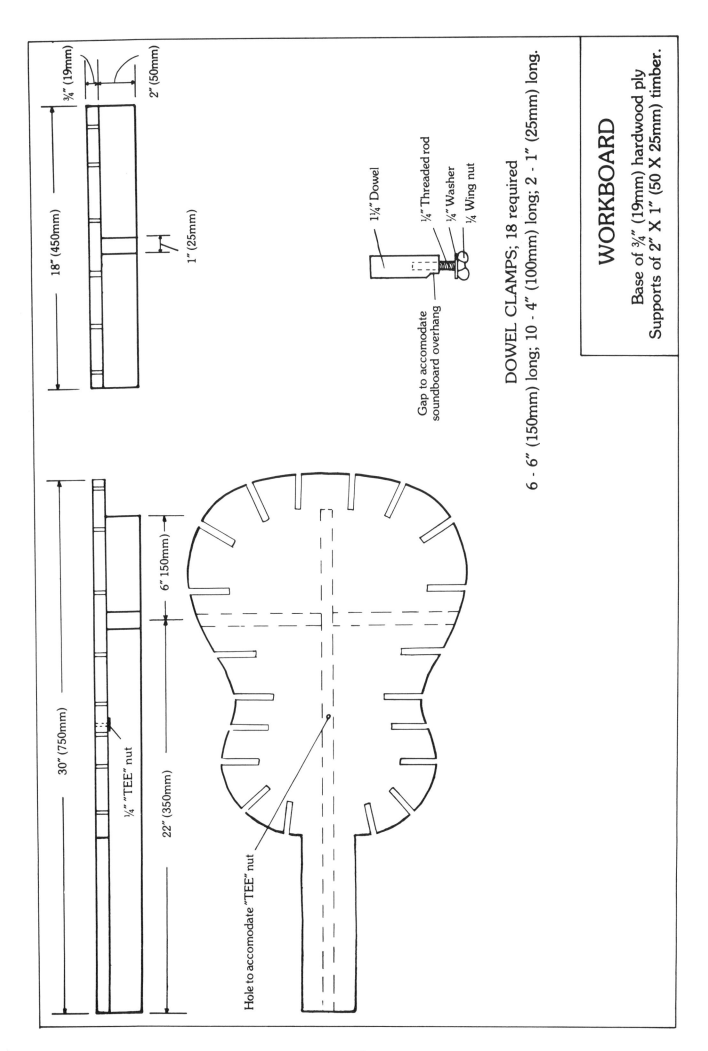

¾" (19mm)

2" (50mm)

18" (450mm)

1" (25mm)

1¼" Dowel

¼" Threaded rod

¼" Washer

¼" Wing nut

Gap to accomodate
soundboard overhang

DOWEL CLAMPS; 18 required

6 - 6" (150mm) long; 10 - 4" (100mm) long; 2 - 1" (25mm) long.

30" (750mm)

¼" "TEE" nut

22" (350mm)

6" 150mm)

Hole to accomodate "TEE" nut

WORKBOARD

Base of ¾" (19mm) hardwood ply
Supports of 2" X 1" (50 X 25mm) timber.

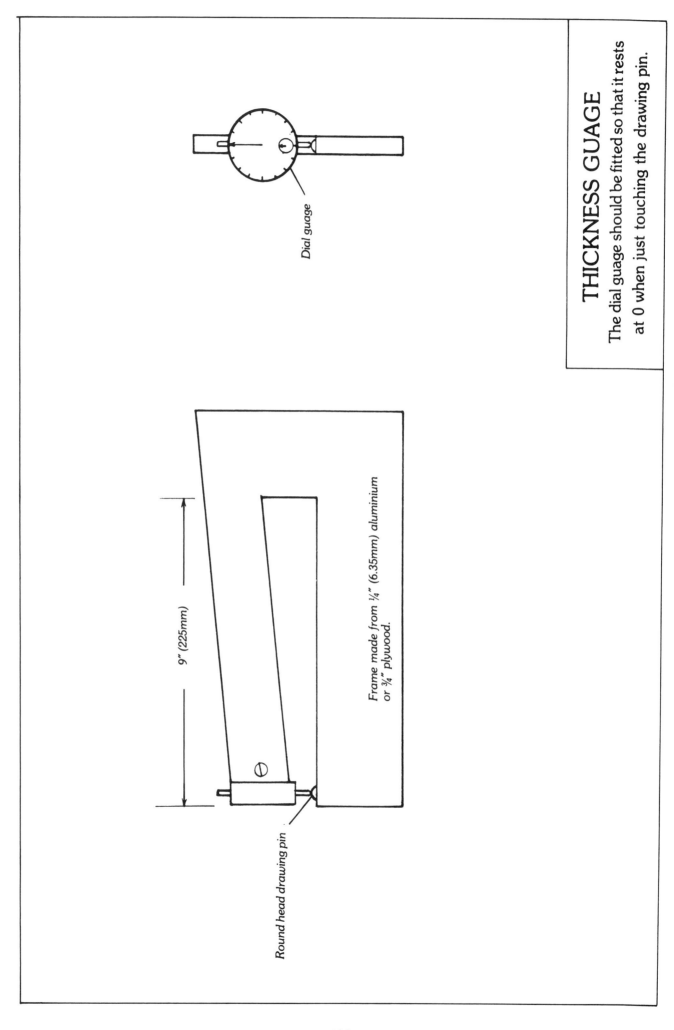

THICKNESS GUAGE

The dial guage should be fitted so that it rests at 0 when just touching the drawing pin.

Dial guage

9" (225mm)

Frame made from ¼" (6.35mm) aluminium or ¾" plywood.

Round head drawing pin

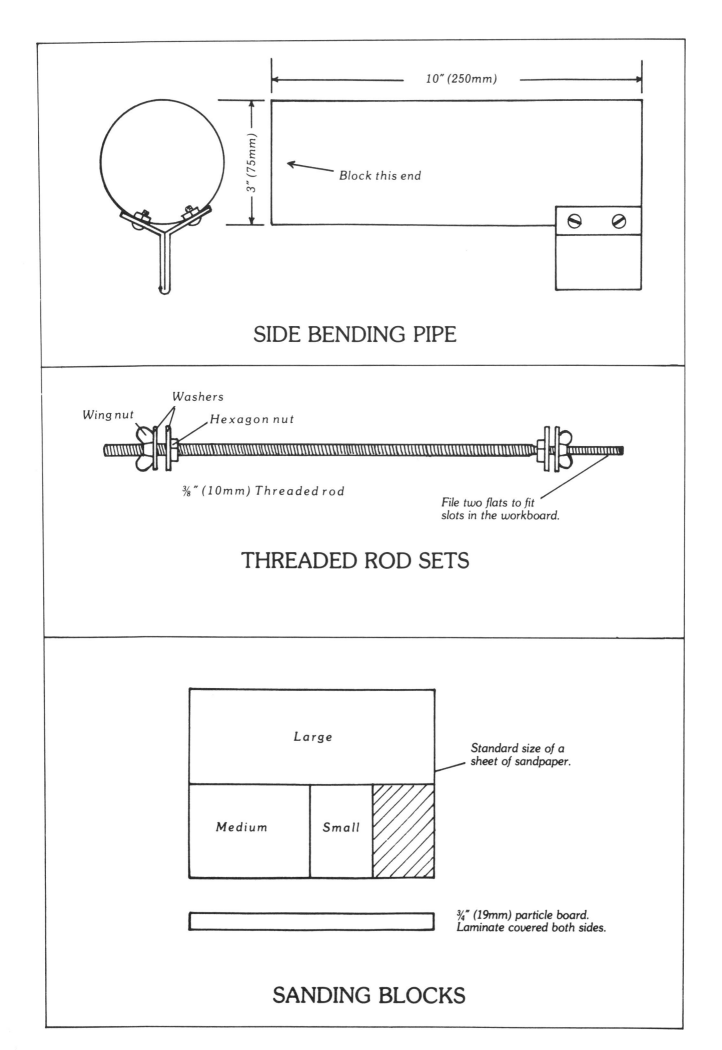

10" (250mm)

3" (75mm)

Block this end

SIDE BENDING PIPE

Wing nut

Washers

Hexagon nut

⅜" (10mm) Threaded rod

File two flats to fit
slots in the workboard.

THREADED ROD SETS

Large

Standard size of a
sheet of sandpaper.

Medium

Small

¾" (19mm) particle board.
Laminate covered both sides.

SANDING BLOCKS

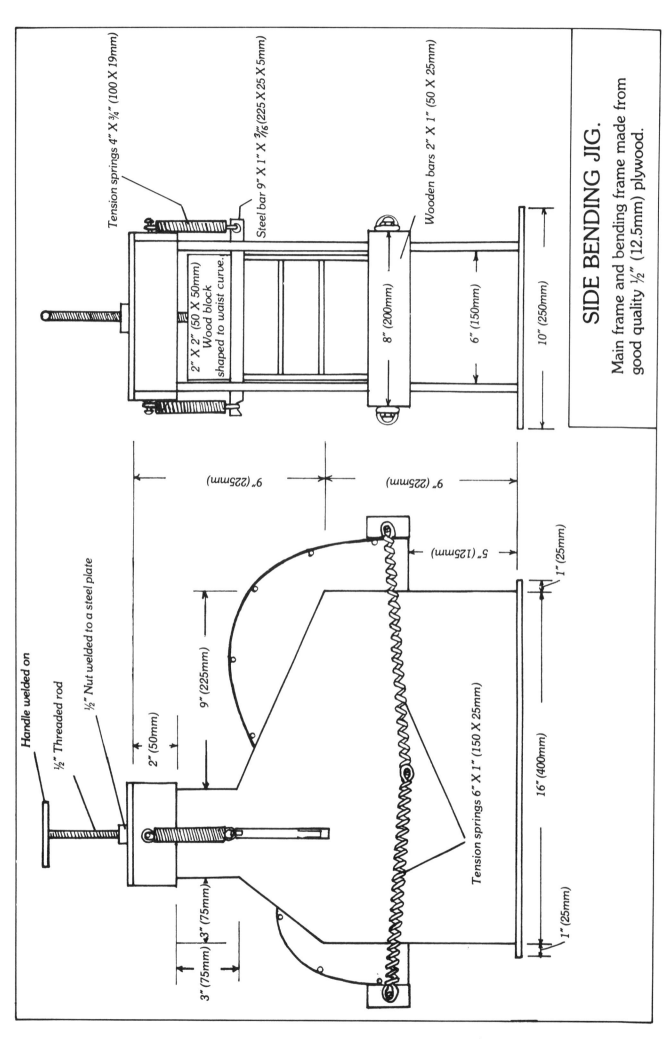

Handle welded on

½" Threaded rod

½" Nut welded to a steel plate

2" (50mm)

9" (225mm)

3" (75mm) 3" (75mm)

Tension springs 6" X 1" (150 X 25mm)

16" (400mm)

1" (25mm)

5" (125mm)

1" (25mm)

9" (225mm)

9" (225mm)

Tension springs 4" X ¾" (100 X 19mm)

Steel bar 9" X 1" X 3⁄16" (225 X 25 X 5mm)

2" X 2" (50 X 50mm) Wood block shaped to waist curve.

Wooden bars 2" X 1" (50 X 25mm)

8" (200mm)

6" (150mm)

10" (250mm)

SIDE BENDING JIG.

Main frame and bending frame made from good quality ½" (12.5mm) plywood.

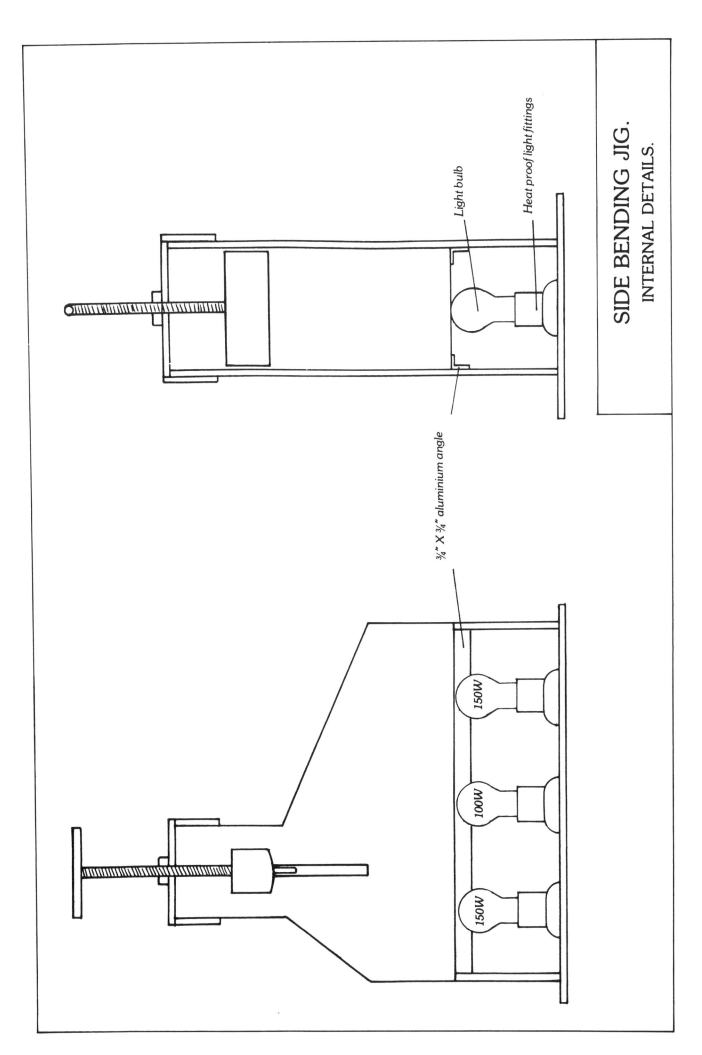

Light bulb

Heat proof light fittings

¾" X ¾" aluminium angle

150W

100W

150W

SIDE BENDING JIG.
INTERNAL DETAILS.

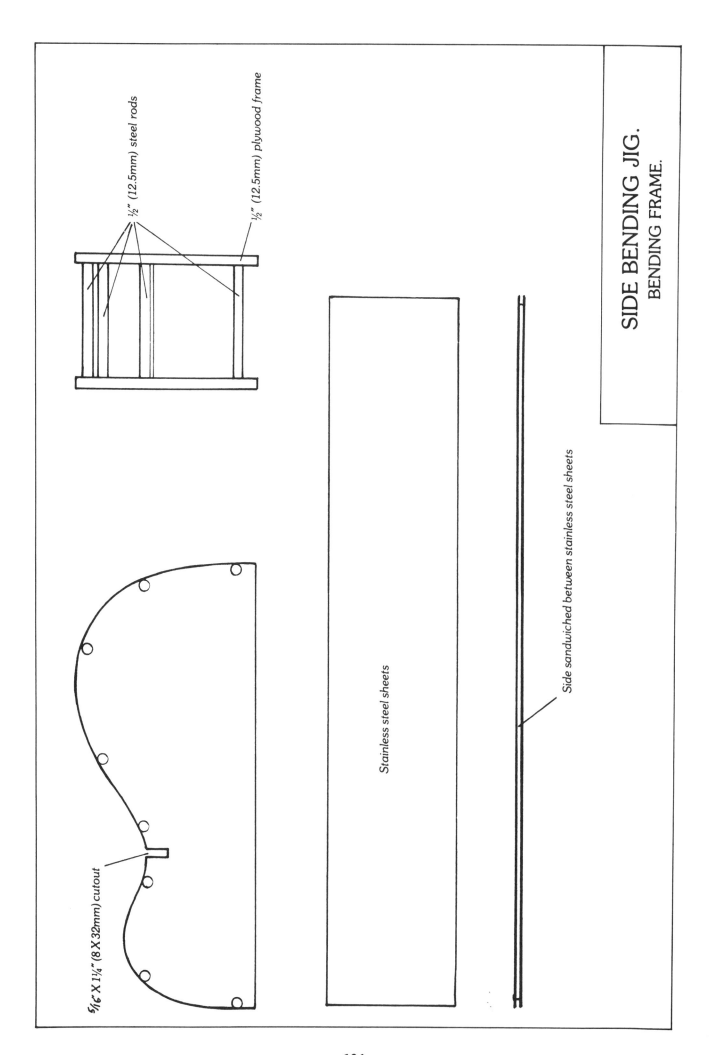

½" (12.5mm) steel rods

½" (12.5mm) plywood frame

⁵⁄₁₆" X 1¼" (8 X 32mm) cutout

Stainless steel sheets

Side sandwiched between stainless steel sheets

SIDE BENDING JIG.
BENDING FRAME.

Template
Diagrams